EAST COAST

Atlantic BEACHES

PHOTOGRAPHS BY

MICHAEL KAHN

SCHIFFER PUBLISHING

4880 Lower Valley Road • Atglen, PA 19310

EXCERPTS

Excerpt from *Letters to a Young Poet* by Rainer Maria Rilke 11
Excerpt from *The Letters of Vincent van Gogh* by Vincent van Gogh 12
"The Surfer" by Christine Yurick 26
Excerpt from "If I Should Have a Daughter" by Sarah Kay 40
Excerpt from "Dance with the Waves" by Christy Ann Martine 54
Excerpt from "For Dudley" by Richard Wilbur 68
Excerpt from "The Waves" by Mary Oliver 82
Excerpt from *Gift from the Sea* by Anne Morrow Lindbergh 96
"A Momentary Creed" by W. S. Merwin 110
Quote by Jacques-Yves Cousteau 124
"Neither Out Far Nor In Deep" by Robert Frost 136

INTRODUCTION

I grew up playing in creeks in southeastern Pennsylvania, spending summers on Topsail Island in North Carolina, and in Maine. I have always been naturally drawn to the water: fishing, swimming, paddling, sailing the Chesapeake Bay. Kind of like a modern-day Huck Finn, I could gather my dog and my fishing rod and spend all day exploring the creeks of my home. When I did attend school, I learned photography. And when I discovered that I was good at it, I started to put the two together: photographing water. My first book, *Brandywine*, was a portfolio of black-and-white photographs of the Brandywine valley, where I grew up. Since then I've moved on to beaches and seascapes of the Atlantic coast, exploring and photographing the beautiful and mysterious ocean and all of its surroundings.

As I grew older, I began to realize that the streams I played in as a child are all connected and eventually flow to the ocean. It became clearer to me that everything we do upstream impacts not just downstream, but the entire globe, of which 71 percent is water. When I put my passion for photography and the outdoors together, I realized how fragile these systems are. The animals of these coastal regions, including birds, fish, and all other wildlife, depend on clean water and open space for their survival.

Whether you live near these beautiful coastal places or are visiting, please remember how important the preservation and conservation of these areas are: not just to us, but to the entire ecosystem of this wonderful planet.

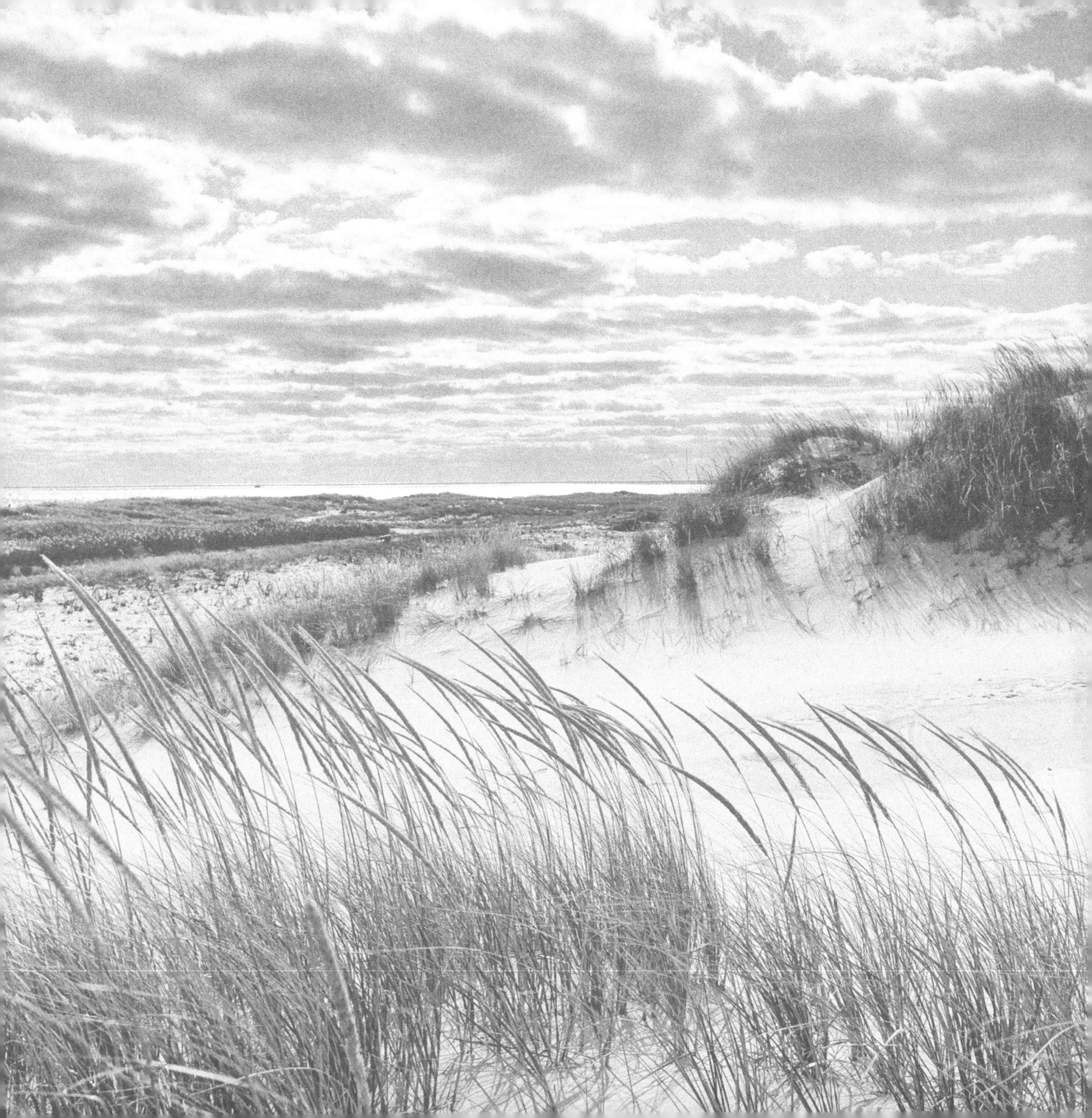

Be patient toward all that is unsolved in your heart and try to love the questions themselves, like locked rooms and like books that are now written in a very foreign tongue. Do not now seek the answers, which cannot be given you because you would not be able to live them. And the point is, to live everything.

—RAINER MARIA RILKE

The heart of man is very much like the sea, it has its storms, it has its tides and in its depths it has its pearls too.

—VINCENT VAN GOGH

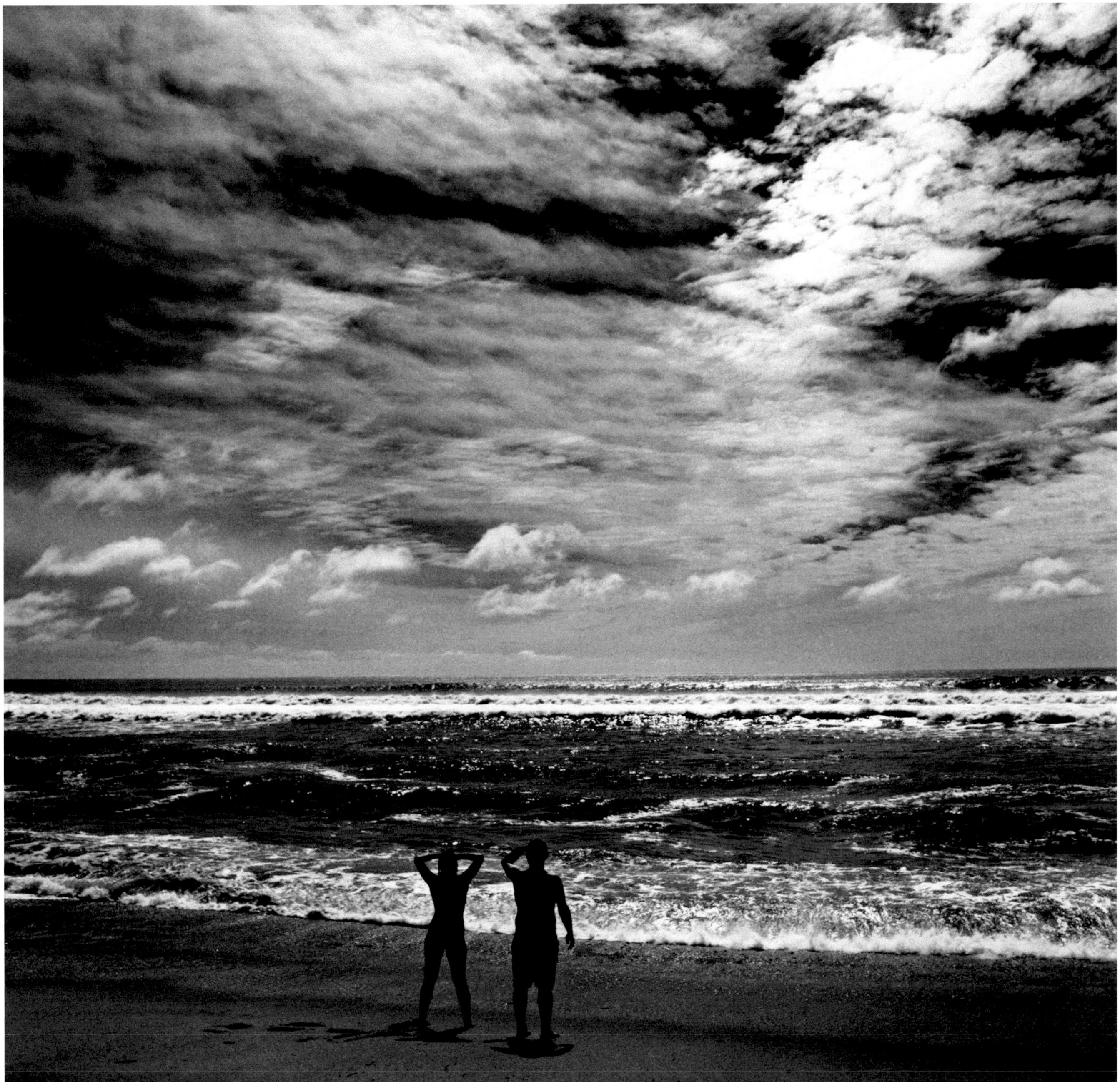

Beach Day, 2011

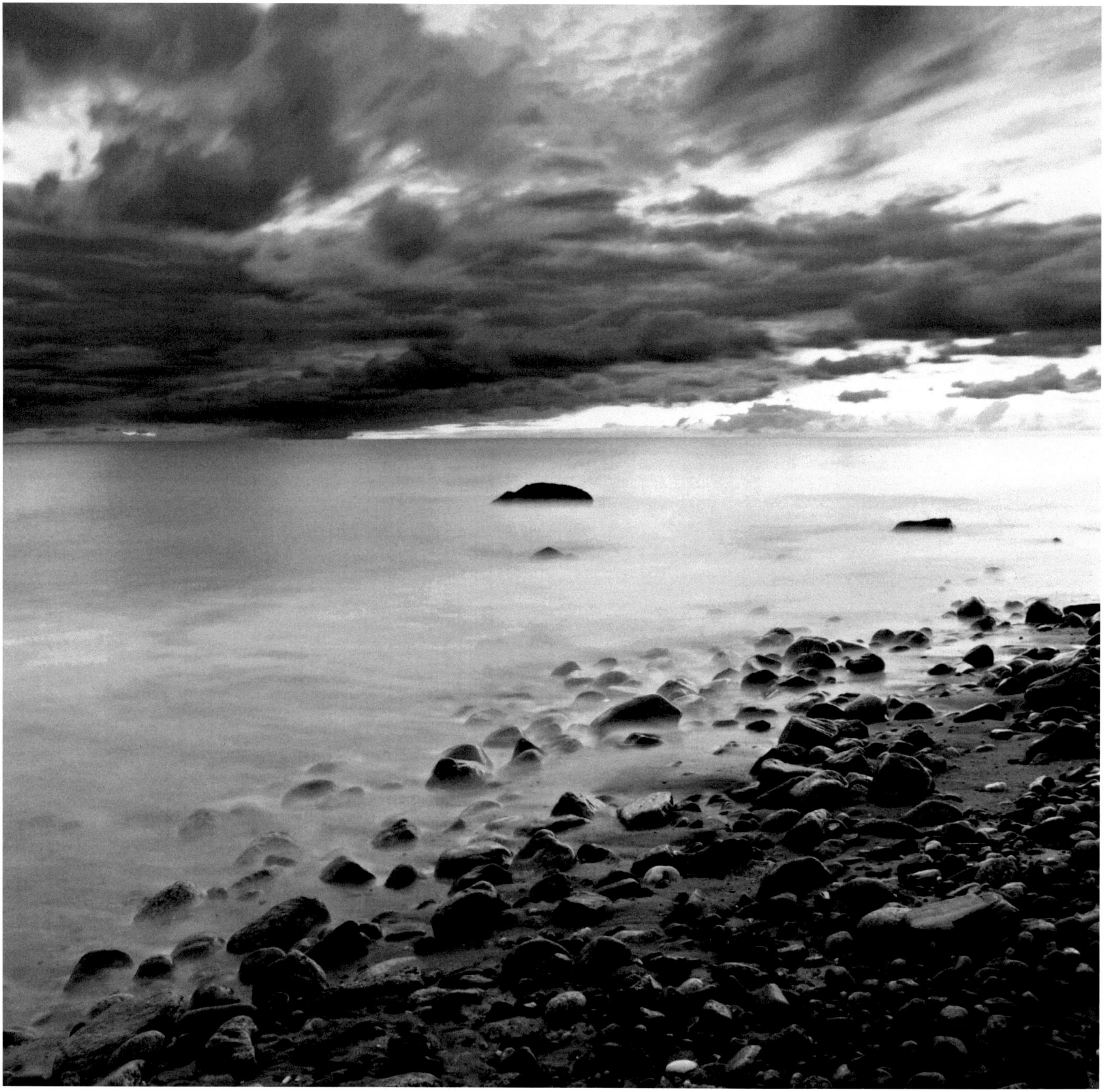

Smooth Seas, 2017

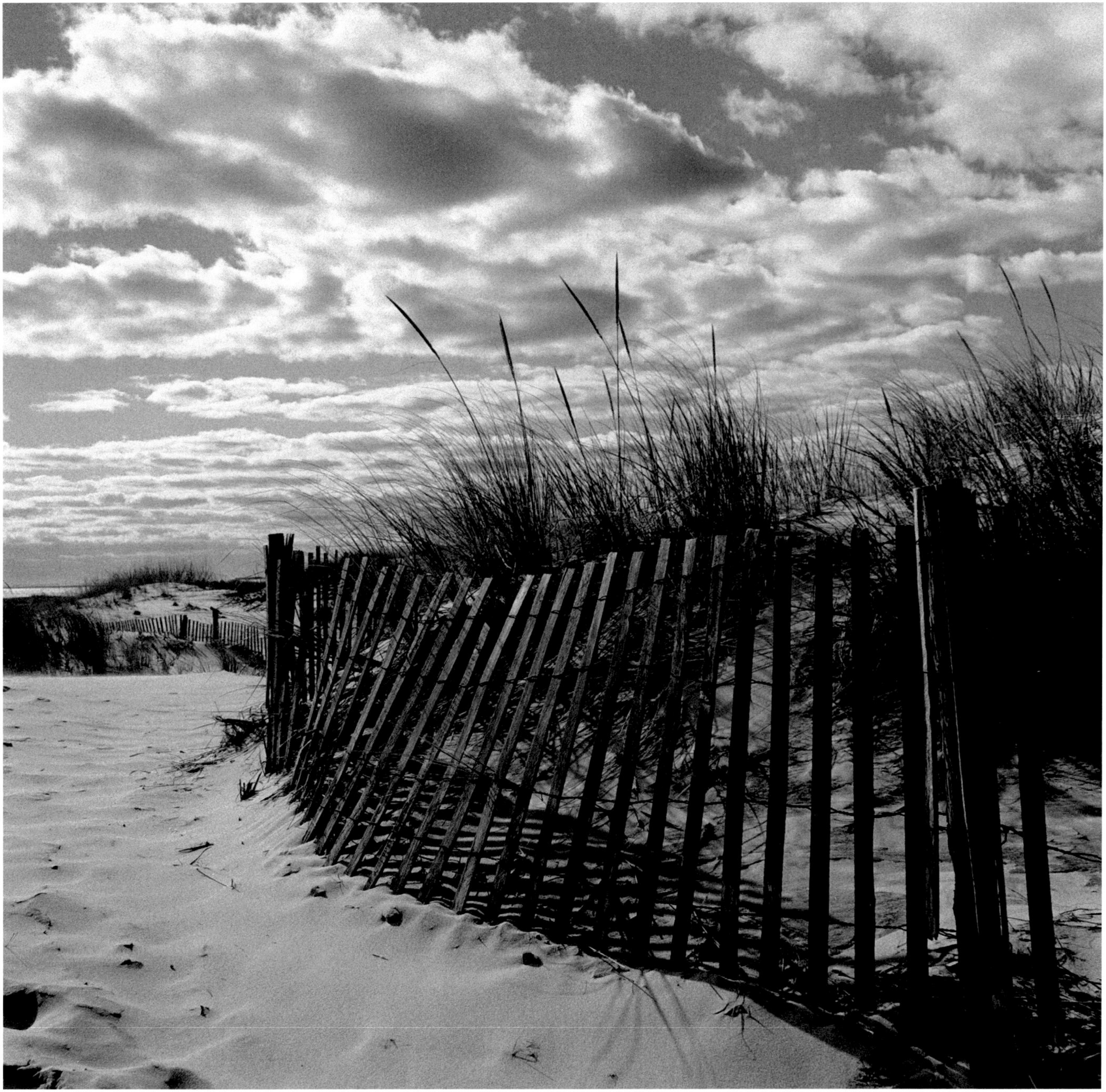

Summer Day, 2008

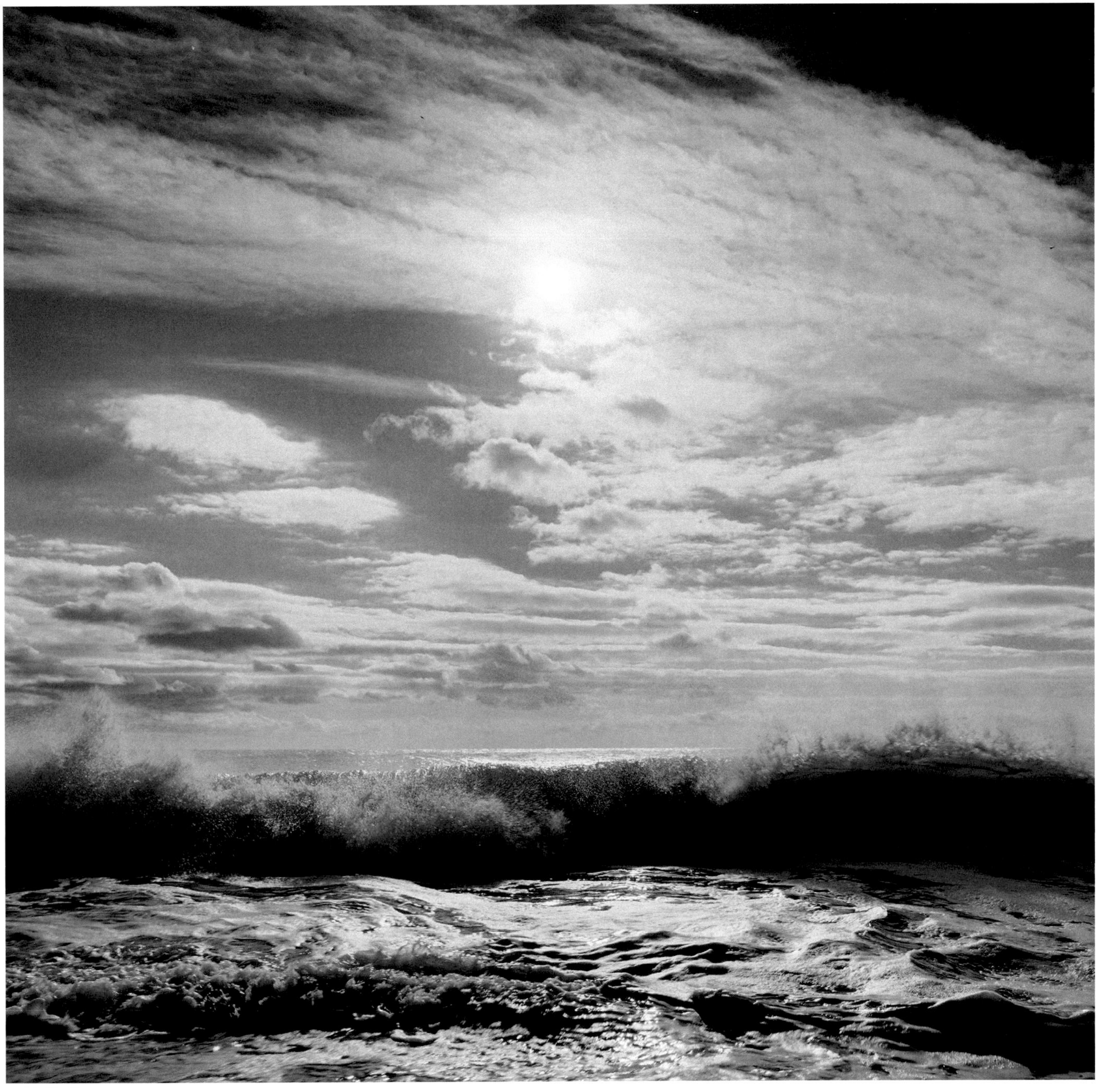

Surf Study, 2017

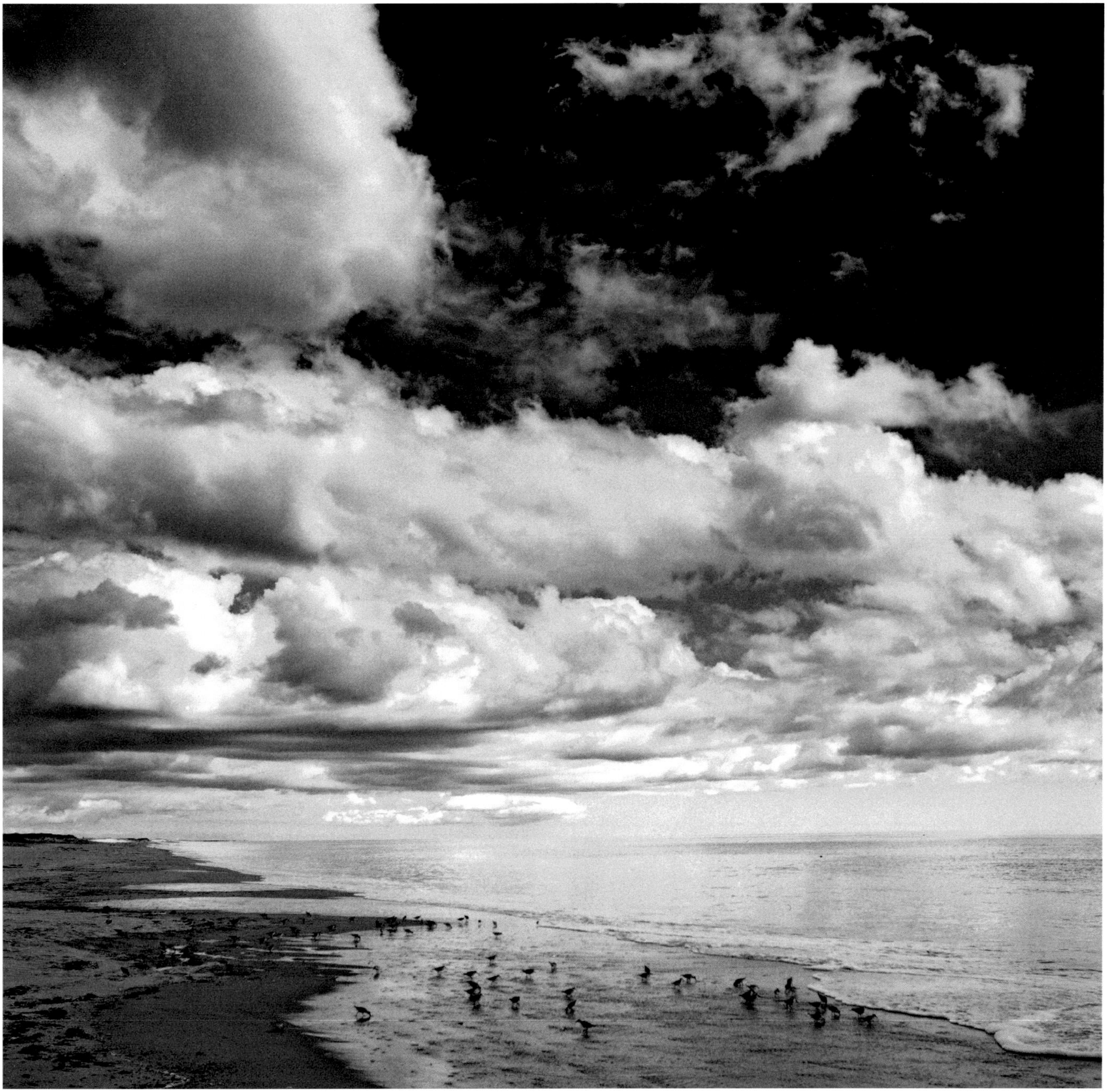

Passing Clouds, 2014

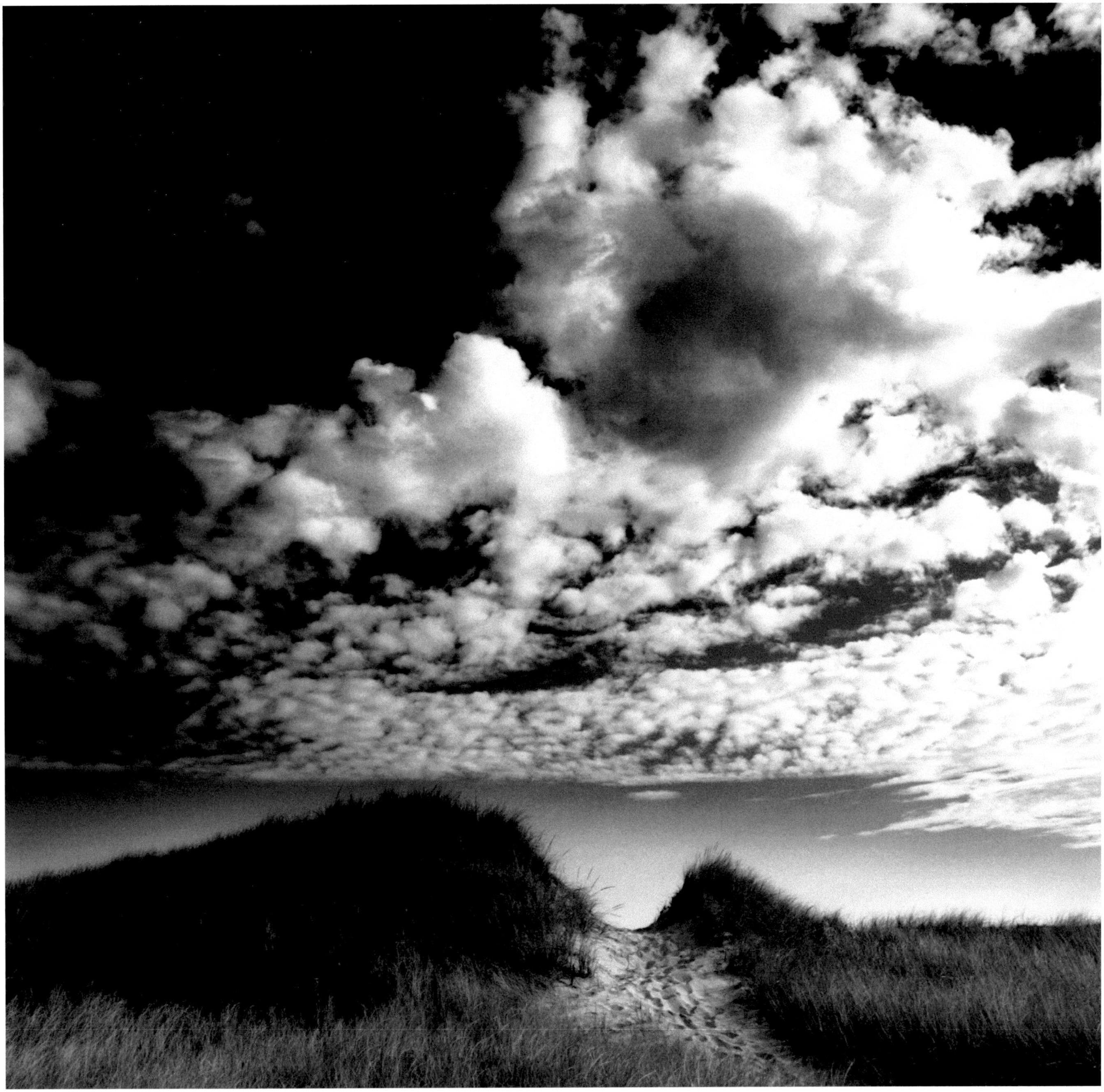

Heading to the Beach, 2011

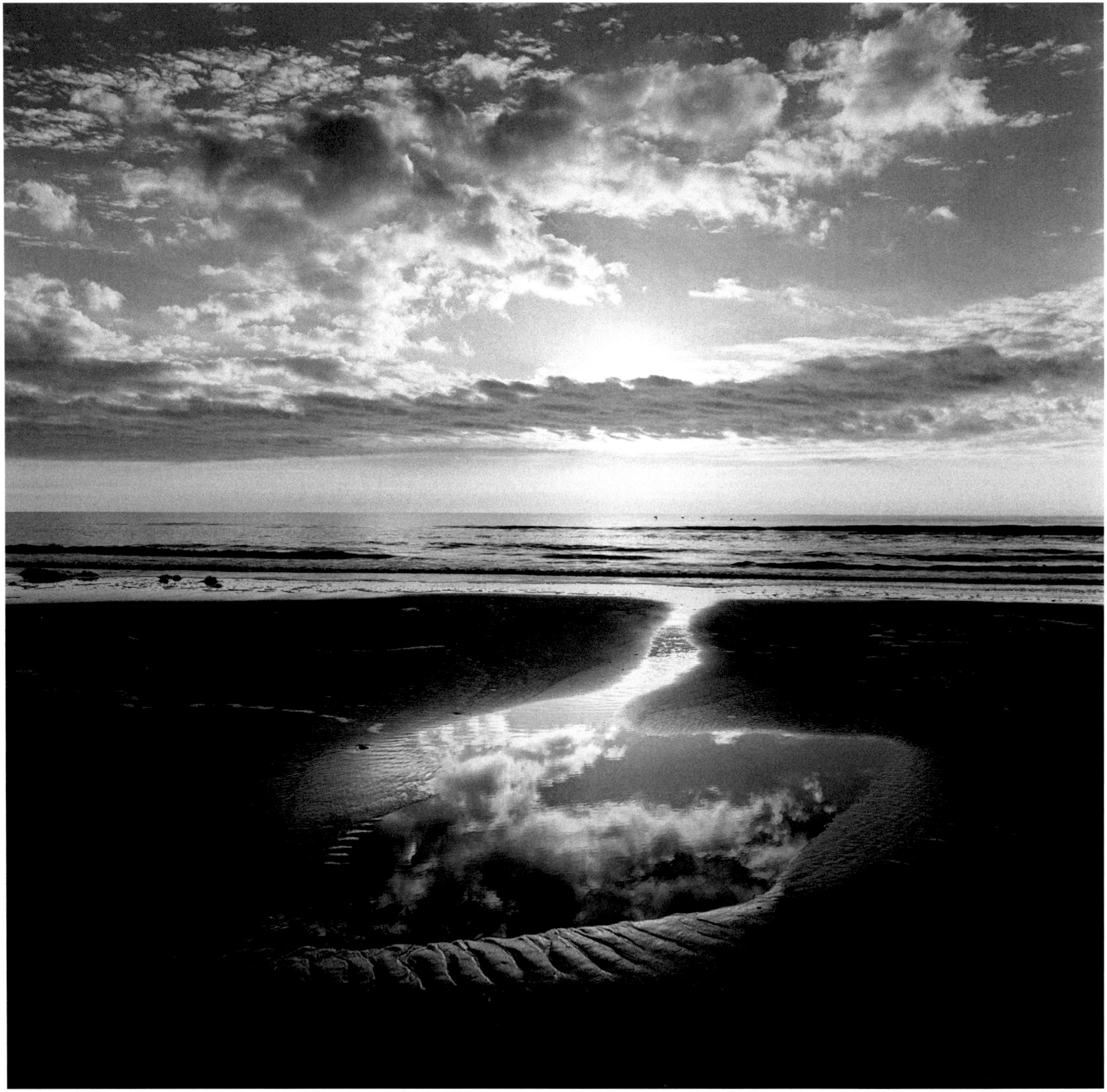

Reflecting Pool, 2007

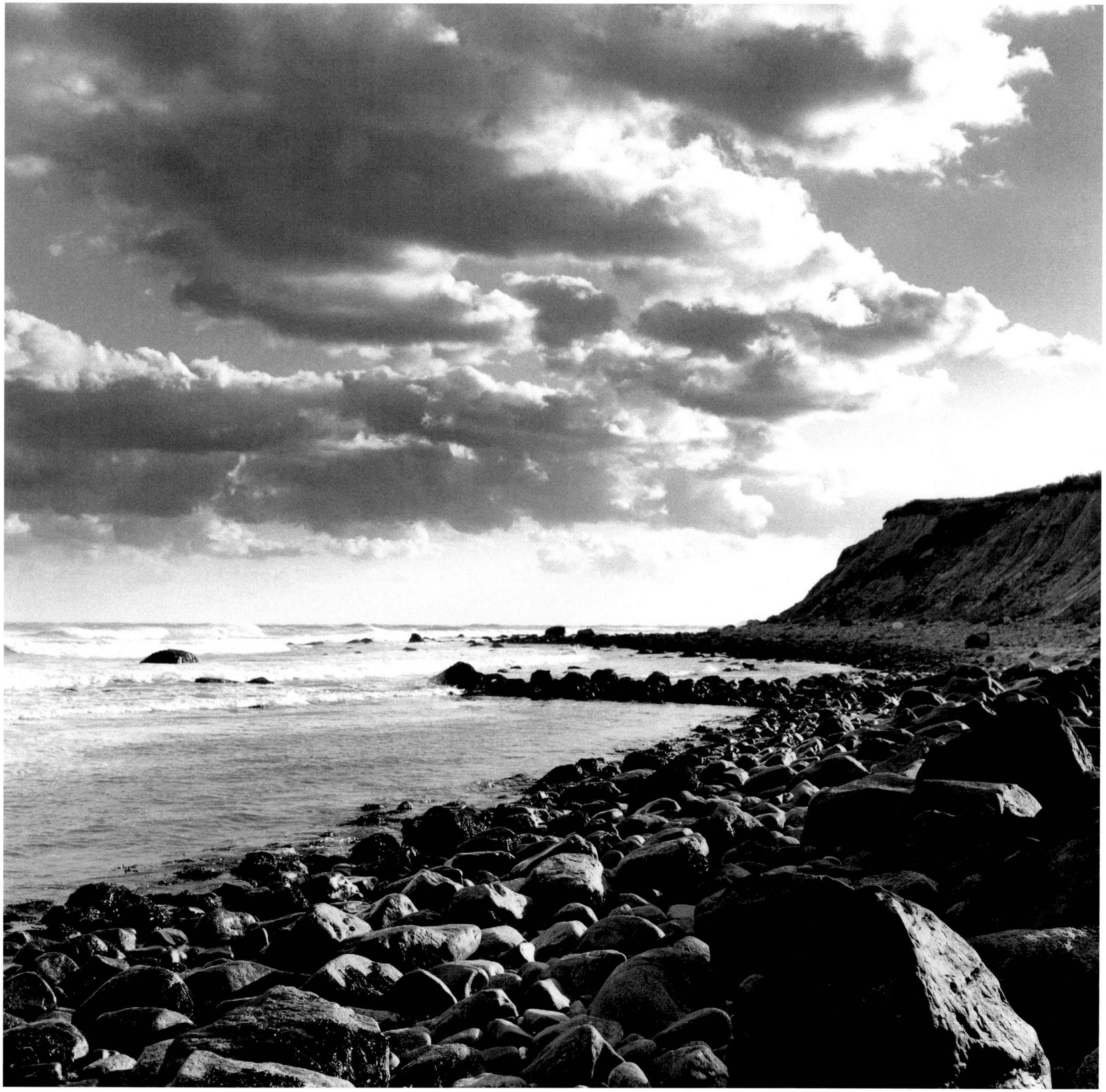

Squibnocket, 2001

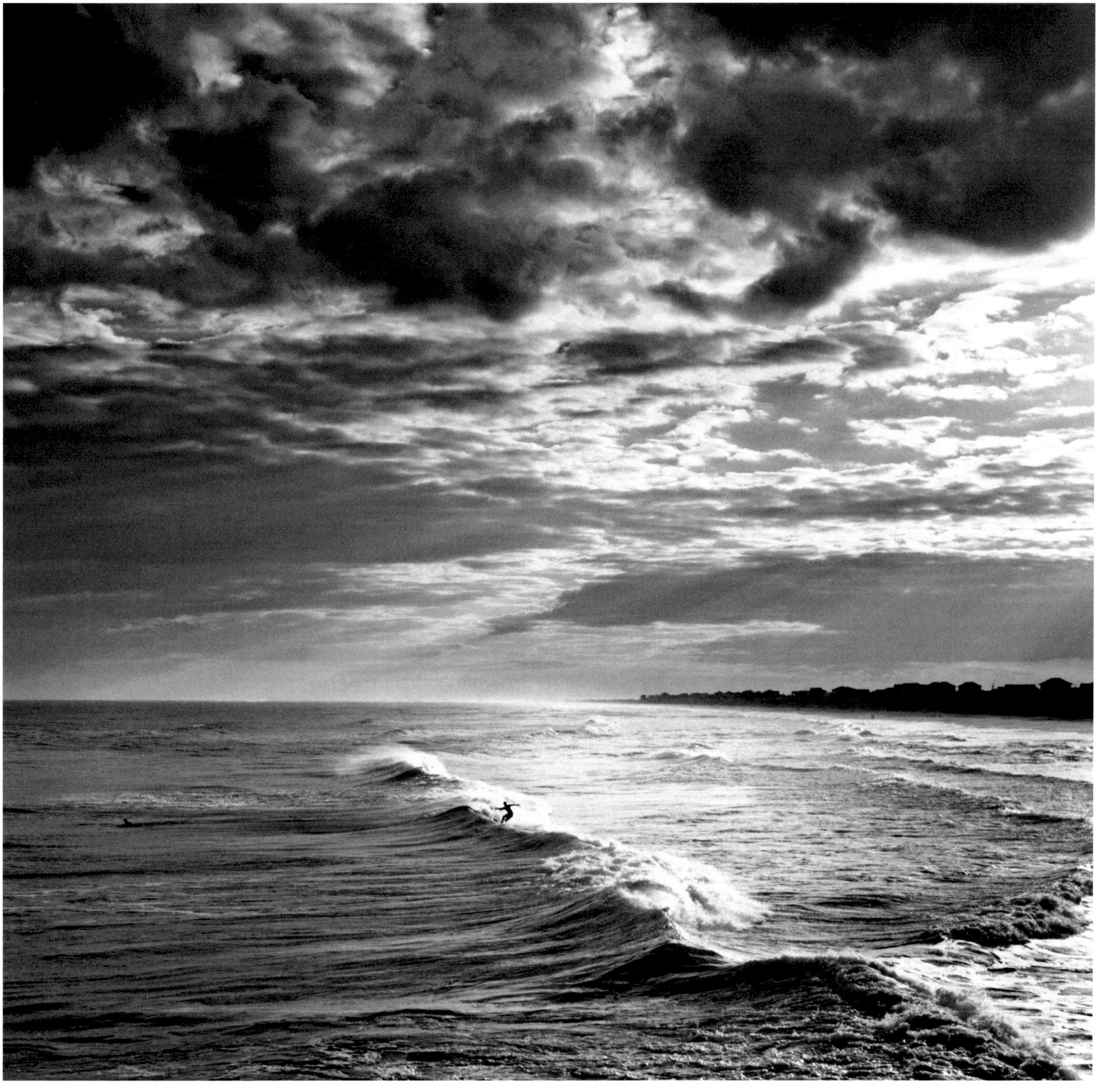

Surfing the Waves, 2014

THE SURFER

Low tide means a mile of what was under water.
A few hours make the difference between a desert
with pine trees rising in mist and islands full of rock and wave.
It is the loudness of the surf that makes the quiet so great.

One surfer sits with his board. He stares at the sea.
What have you come for? The sea asks. *To master your power*,
the surfer replies. *And what do you know of my power*,
the moon intercedes. *Well*, the surfer hesitates,
then points at a seagull, *The seagull flies in wind and dives*
into your body to get its food, he stops, then looks up at the clouds.
The bird doesn't think, and neither should I, the surfer says.
Then he smiles and rides the waves and is no more.

—CHRISTINE YURICK

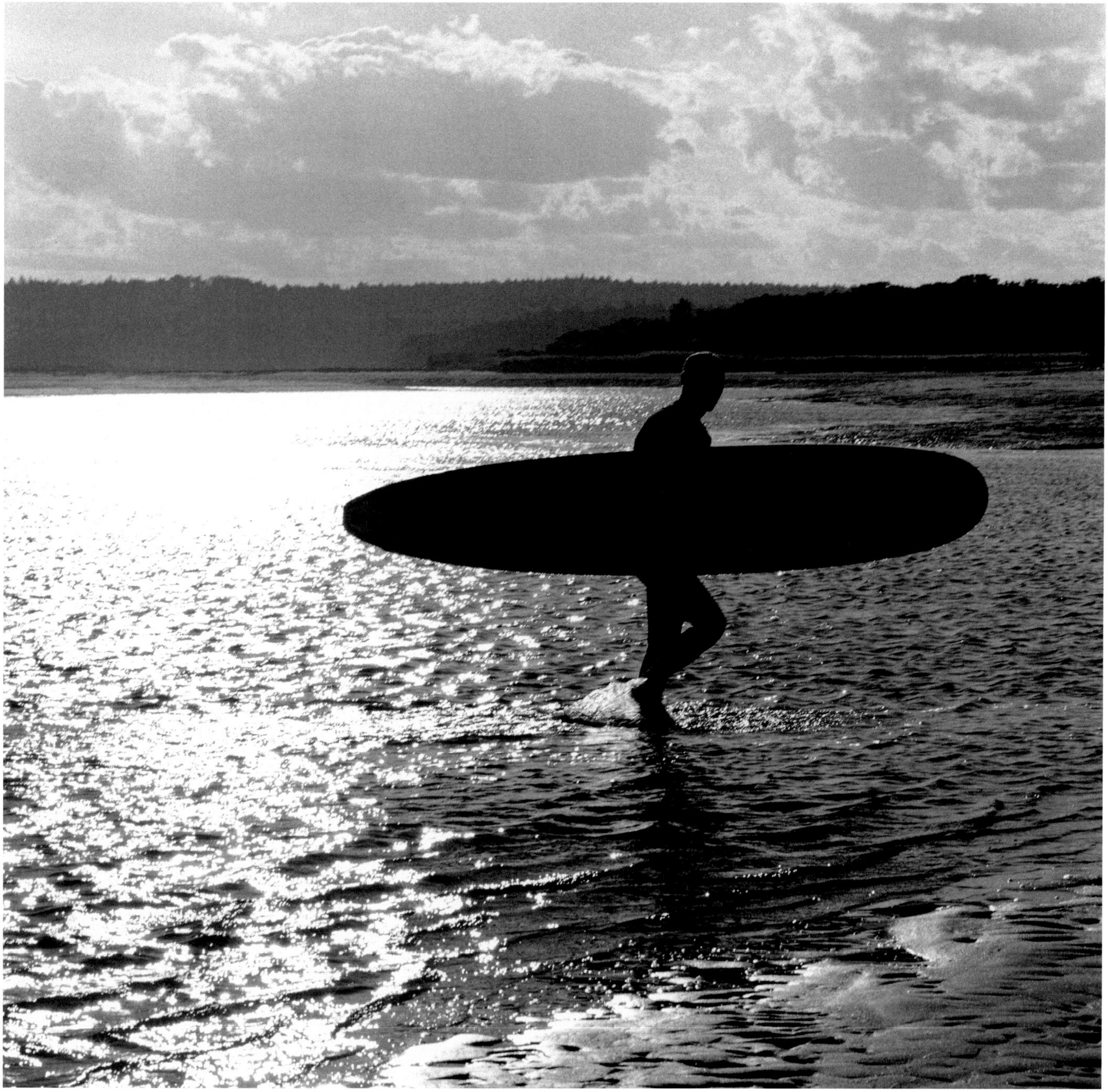

The Surfer, 2006

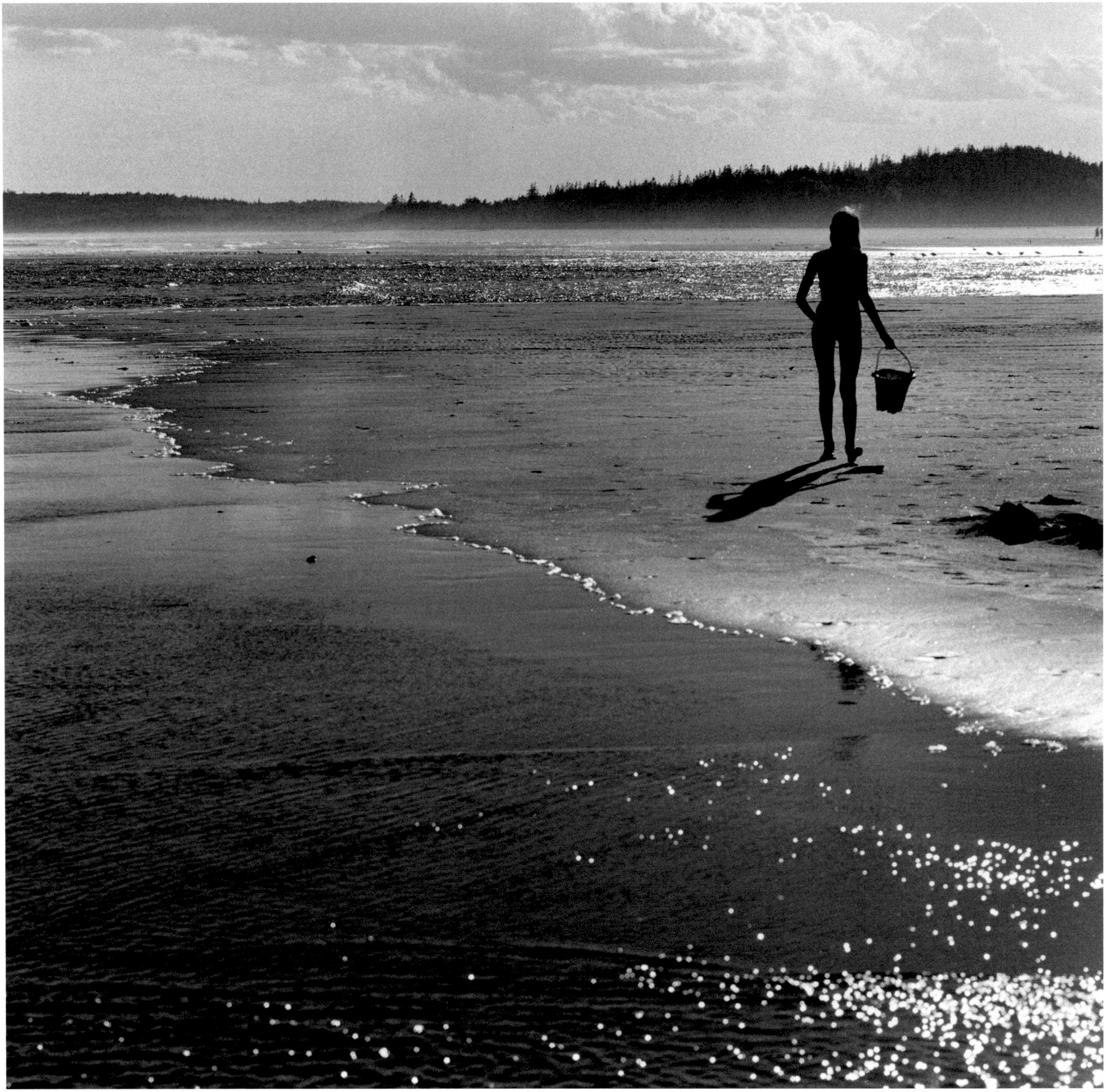

Building Sand Castles, 2006

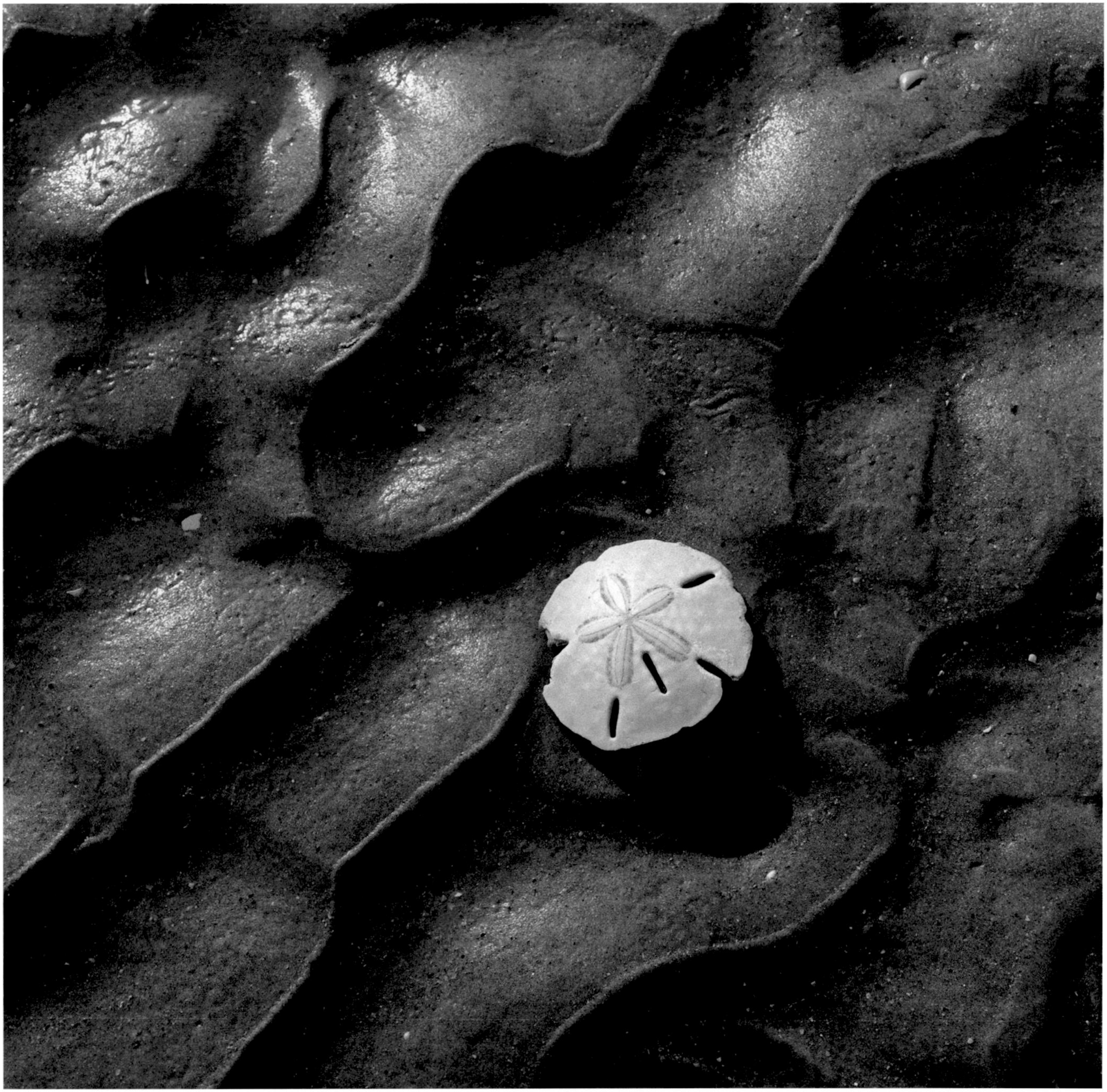

Sand Dollar, 2007

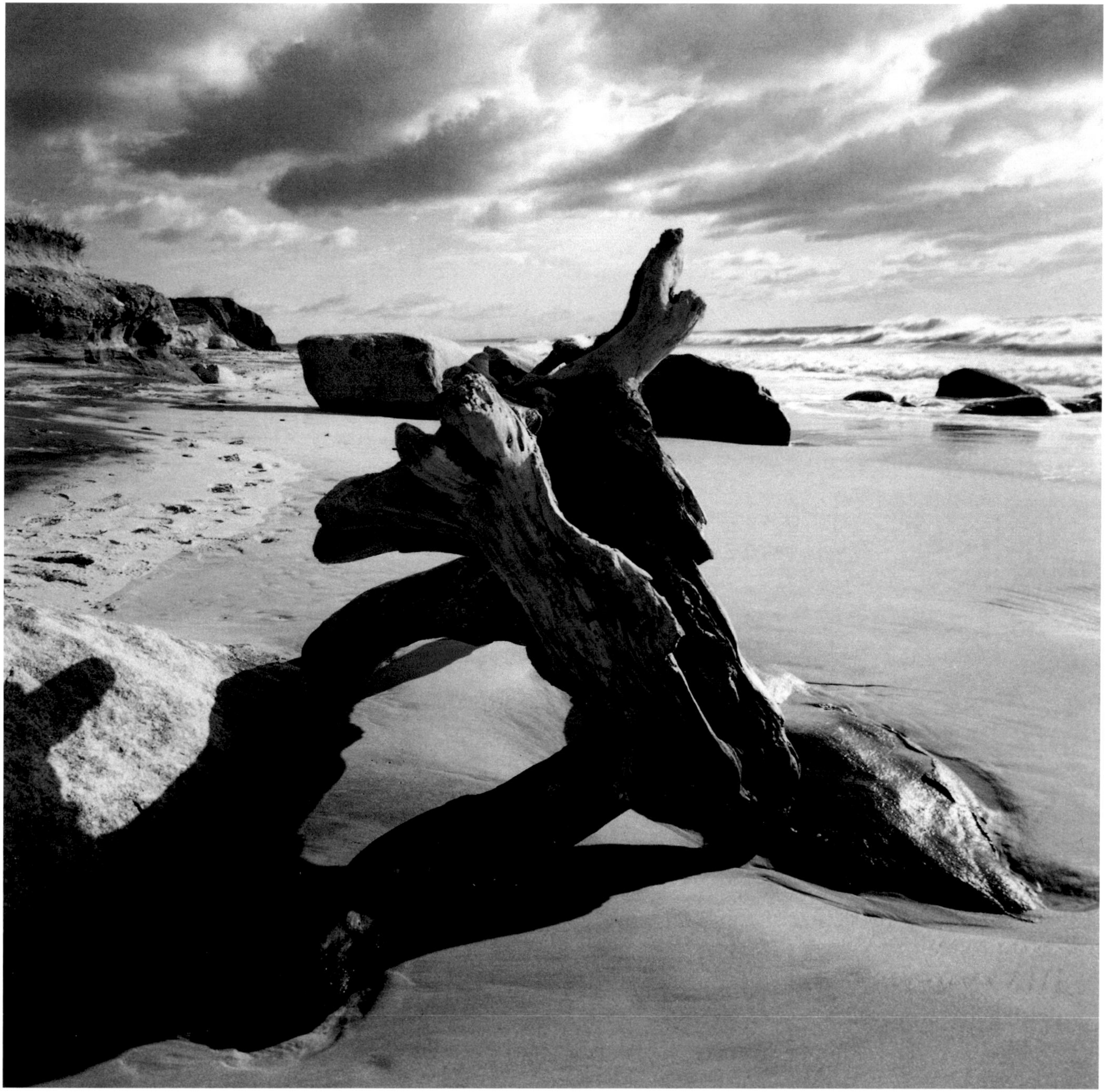

Driftwood, Lucy Vincent Beach, 2003

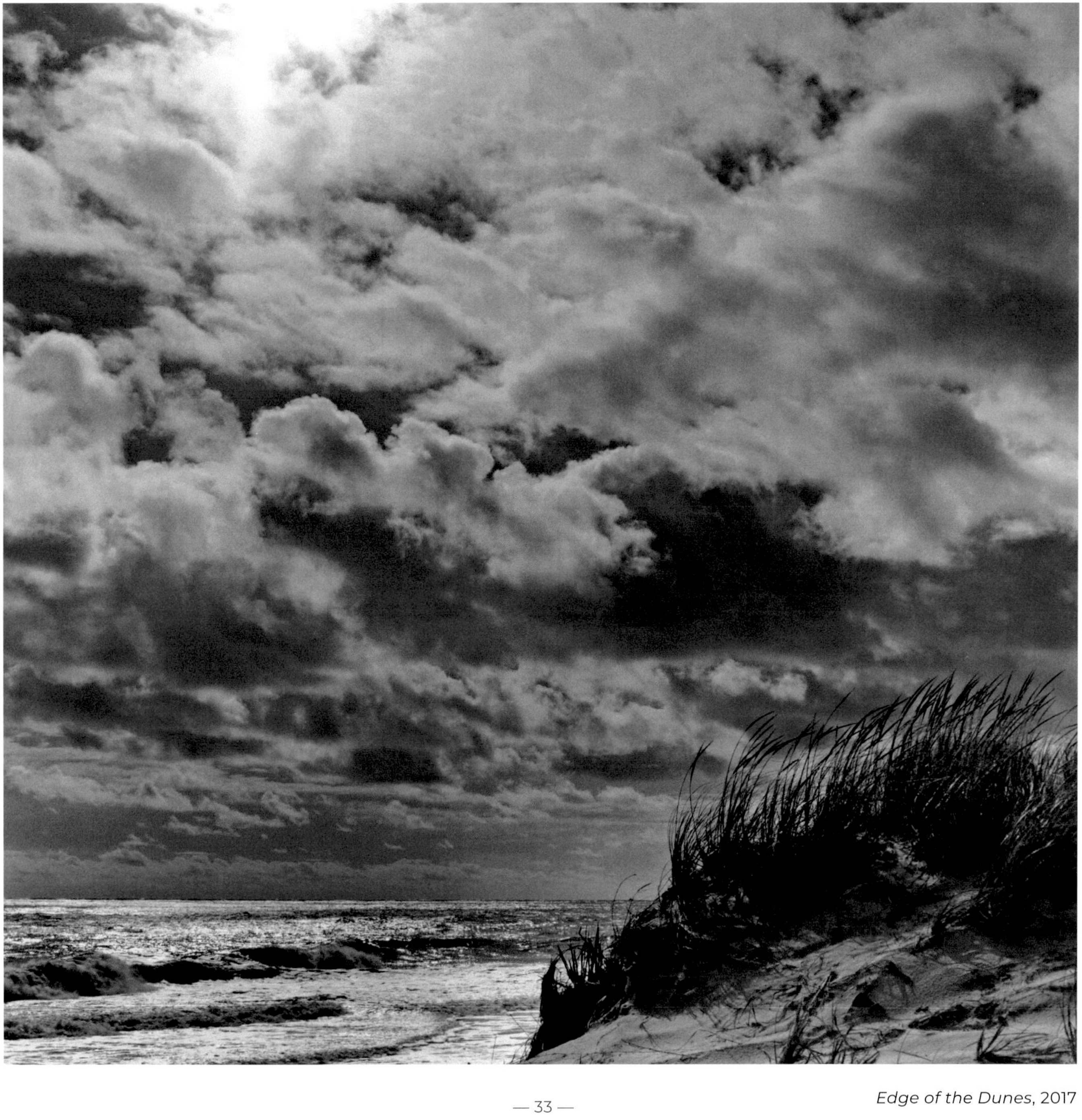

Edge of the Dunes, 2017

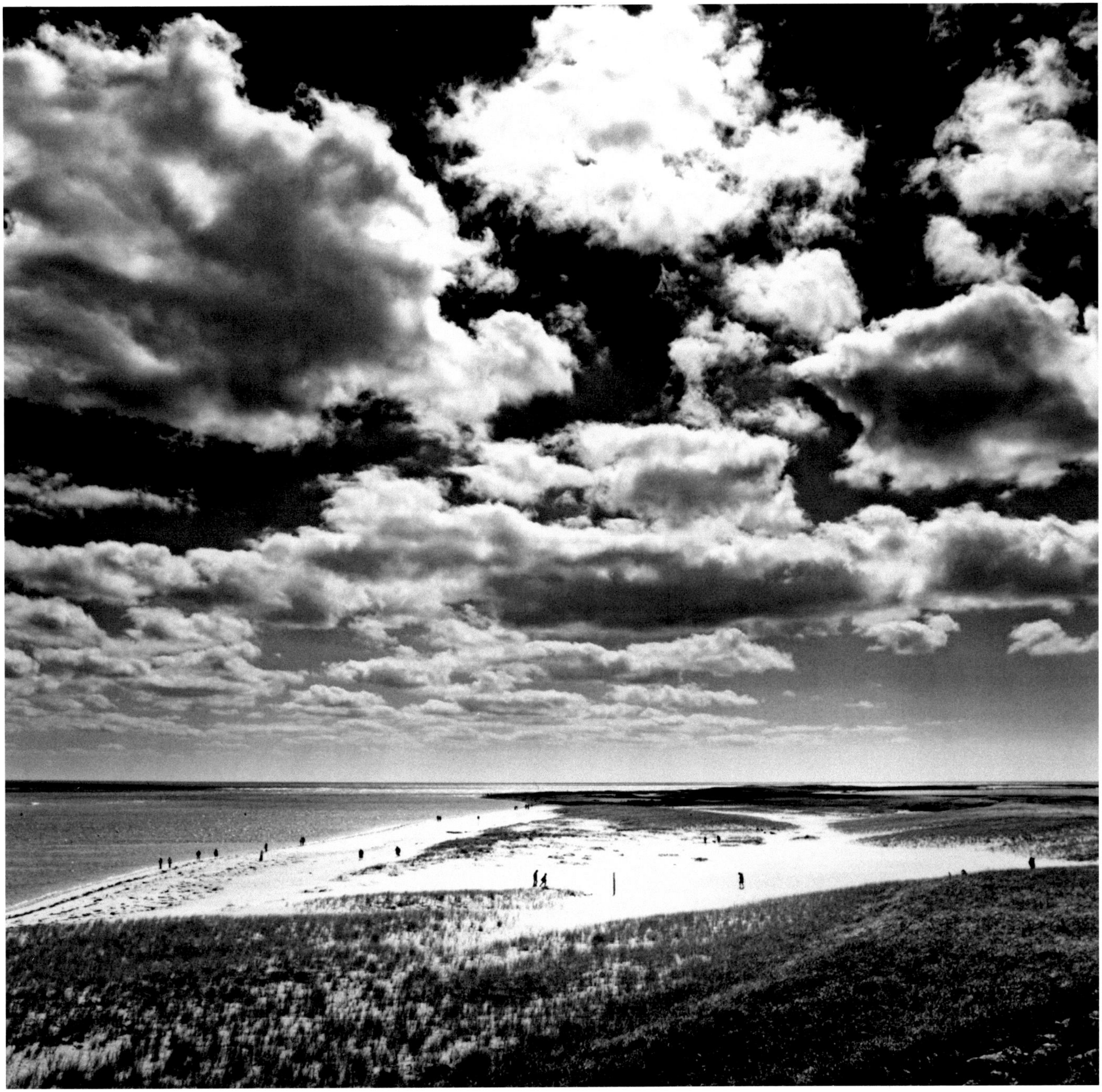

Chatham Inlet, 2014

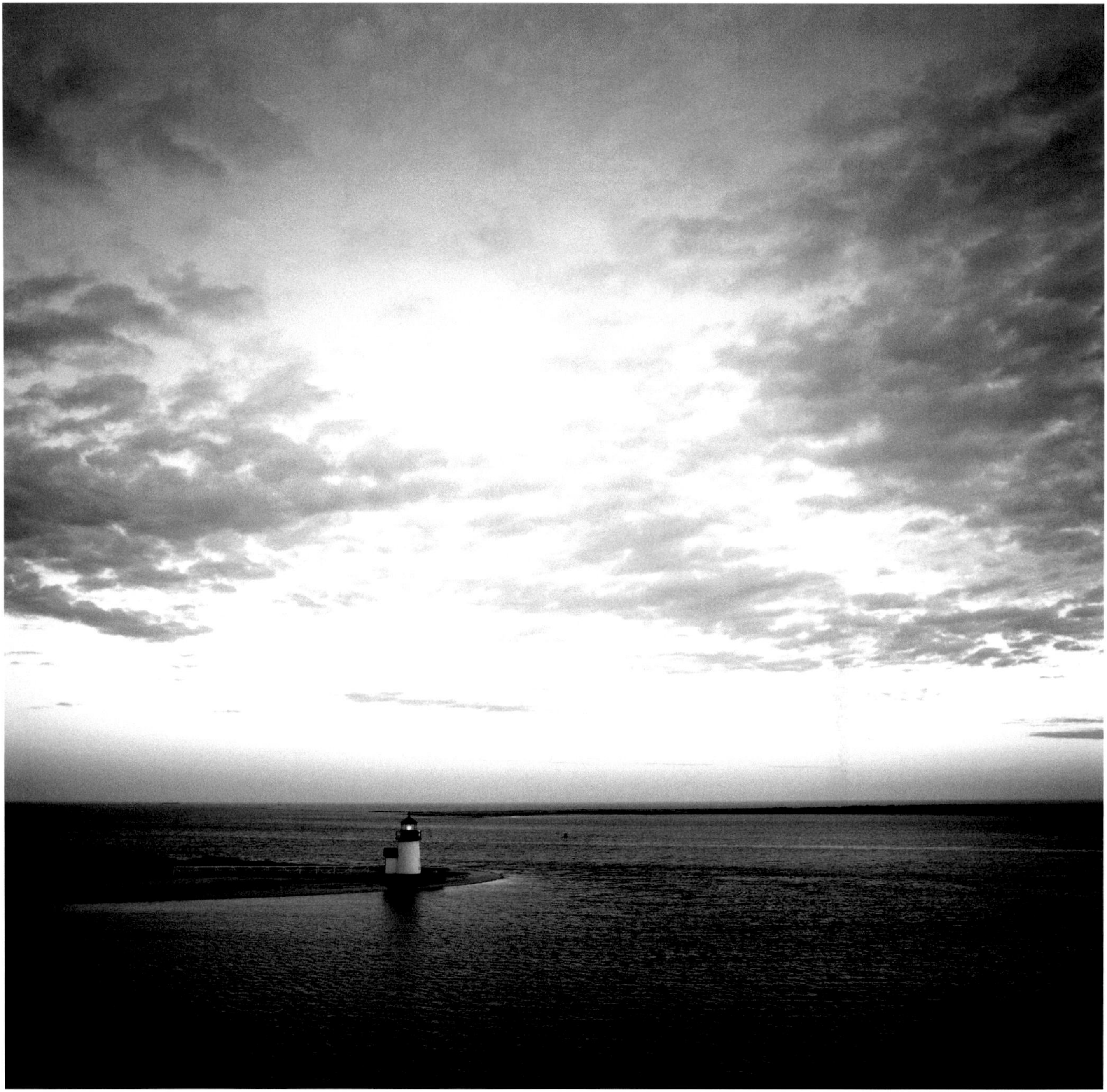

Brant Point Light, Nantucket, 2005

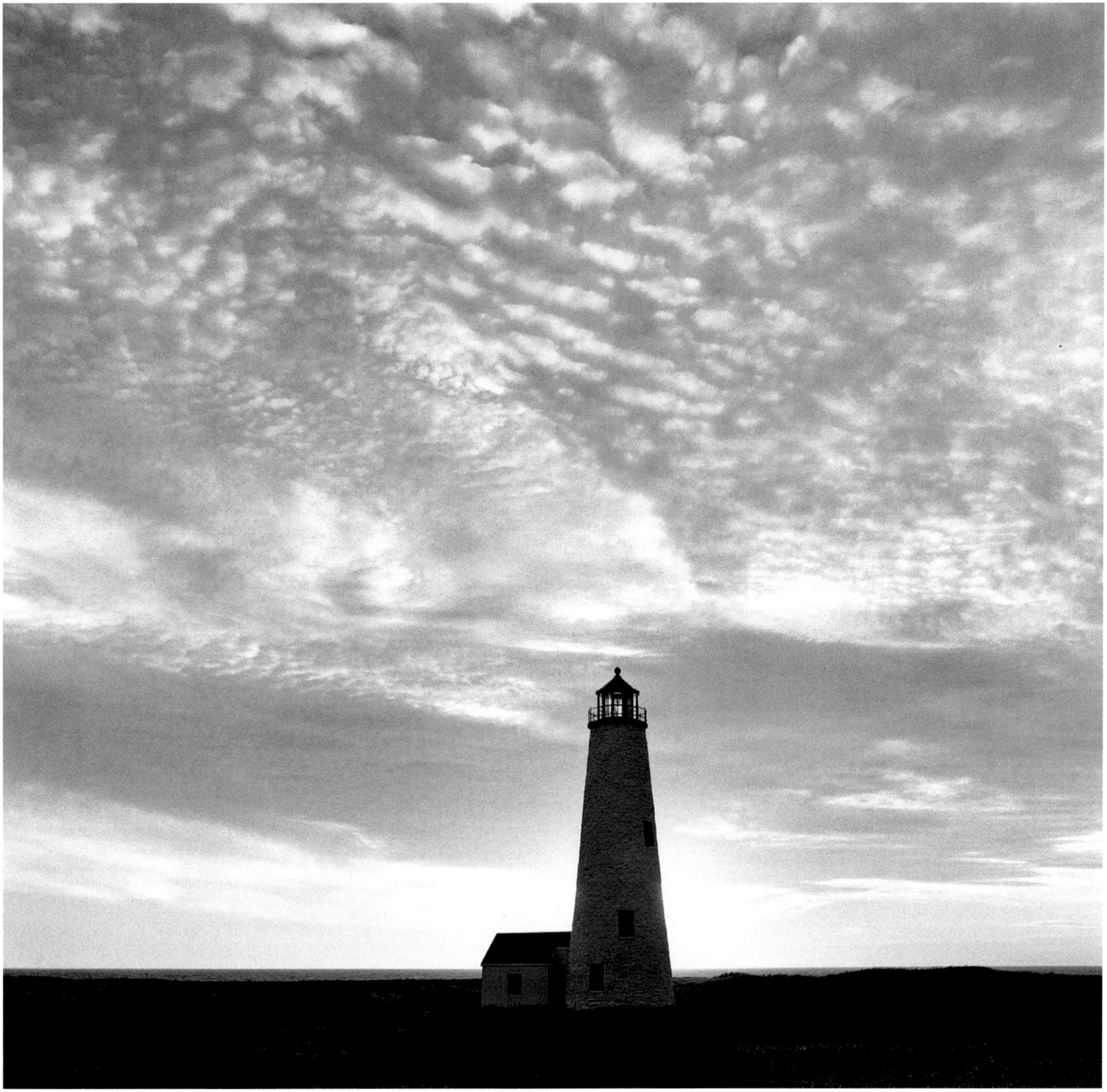

Great Point Light, Nantucket, 2006

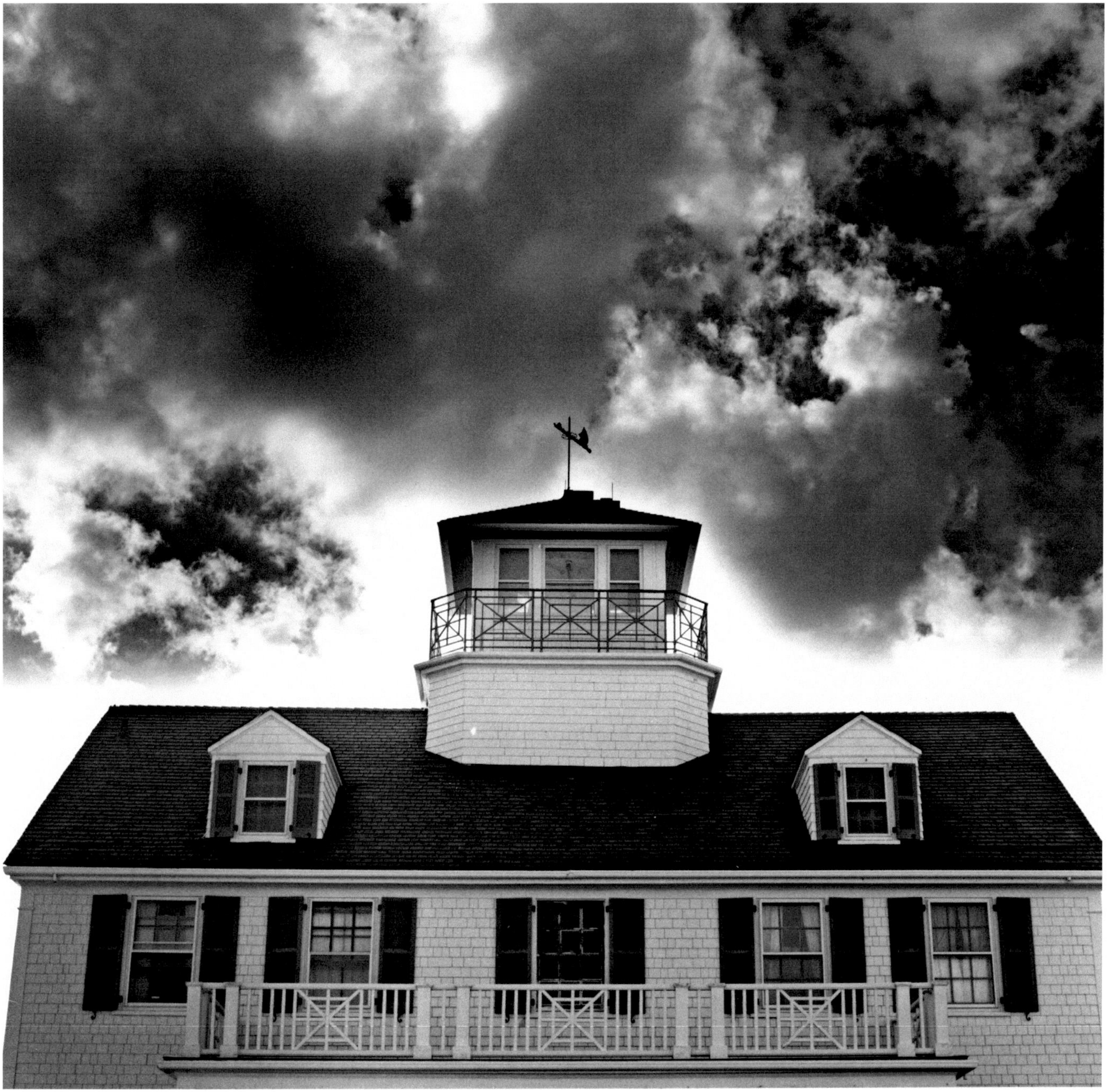

Coast Guard Station, 2014

Because there's nothing more beautiful than the way the ocean refuses to stop kissing the shoreline, no matter how many times it's sent away.

—SARAH KAY

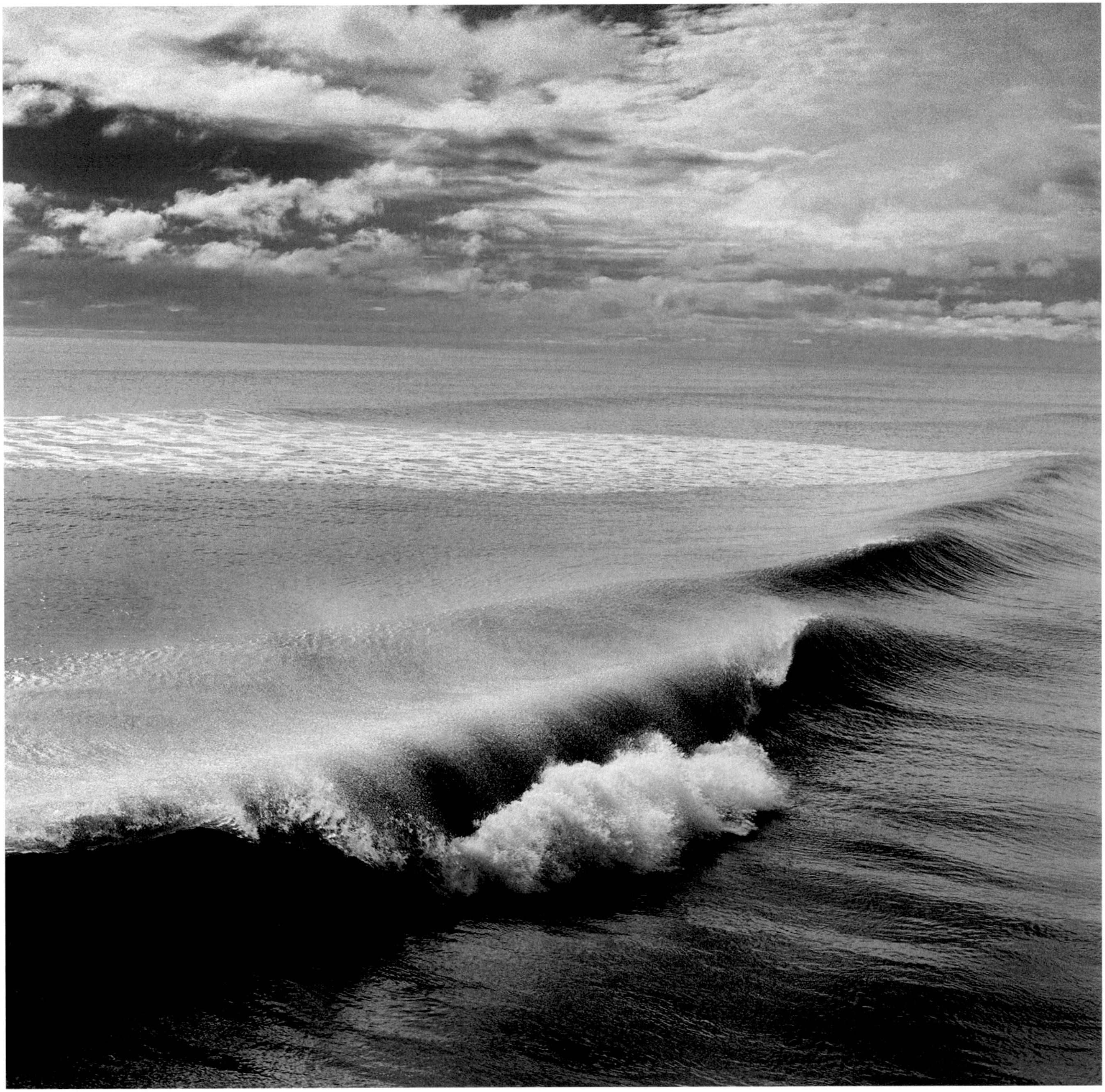

Wave Study, 2006

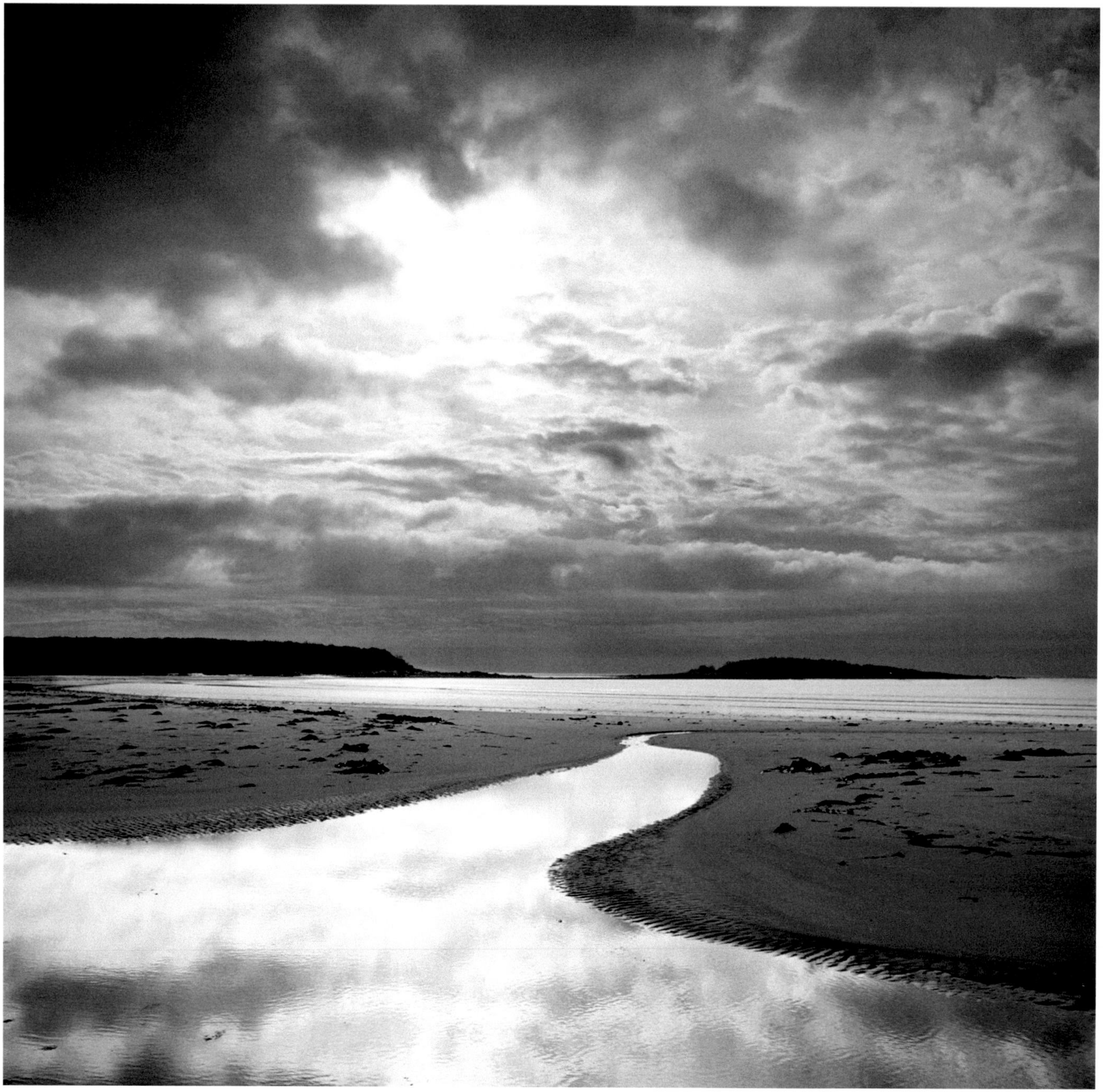

Goose Rocks Beach, 2005

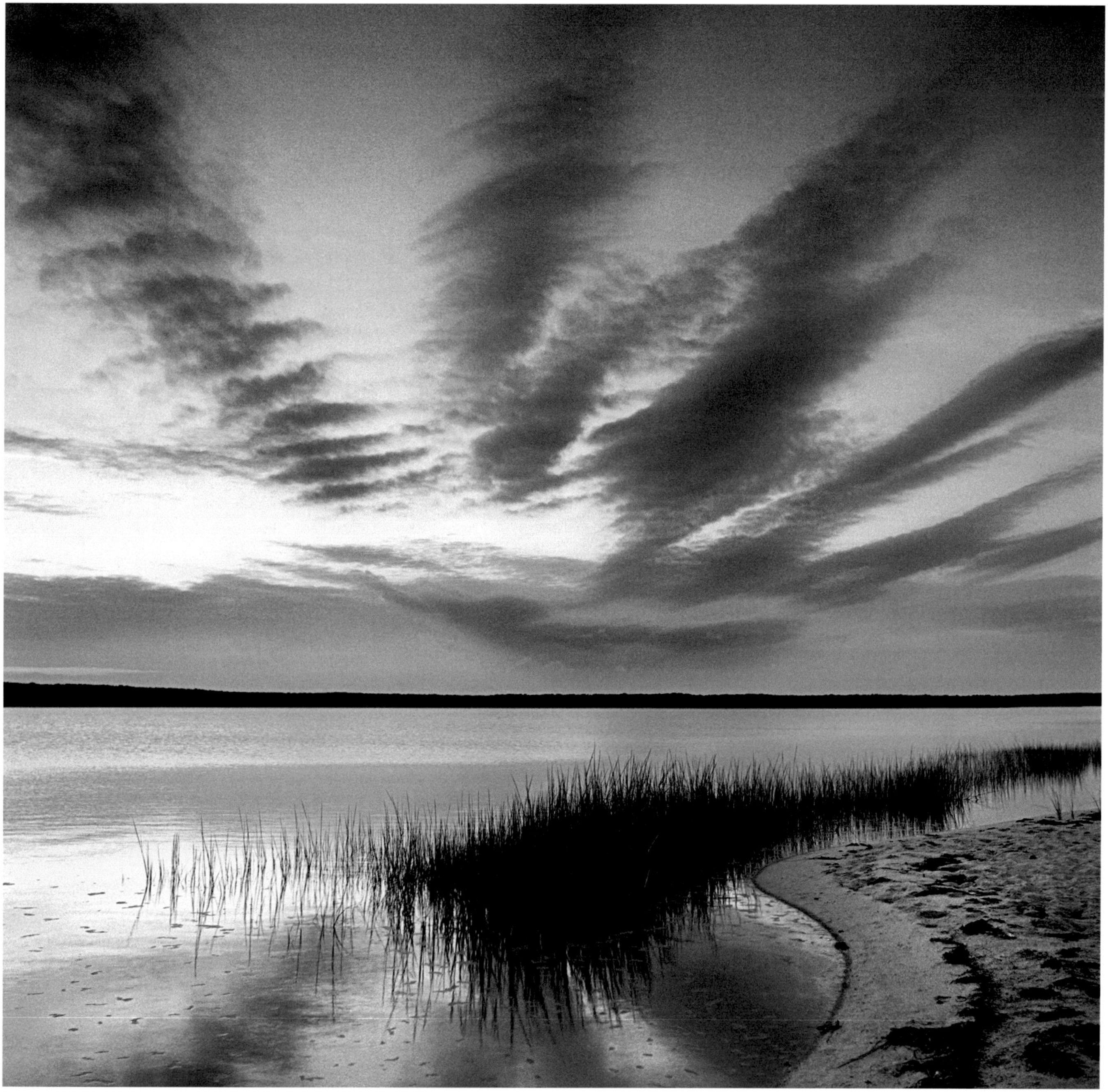

Pocha Pond, 1998

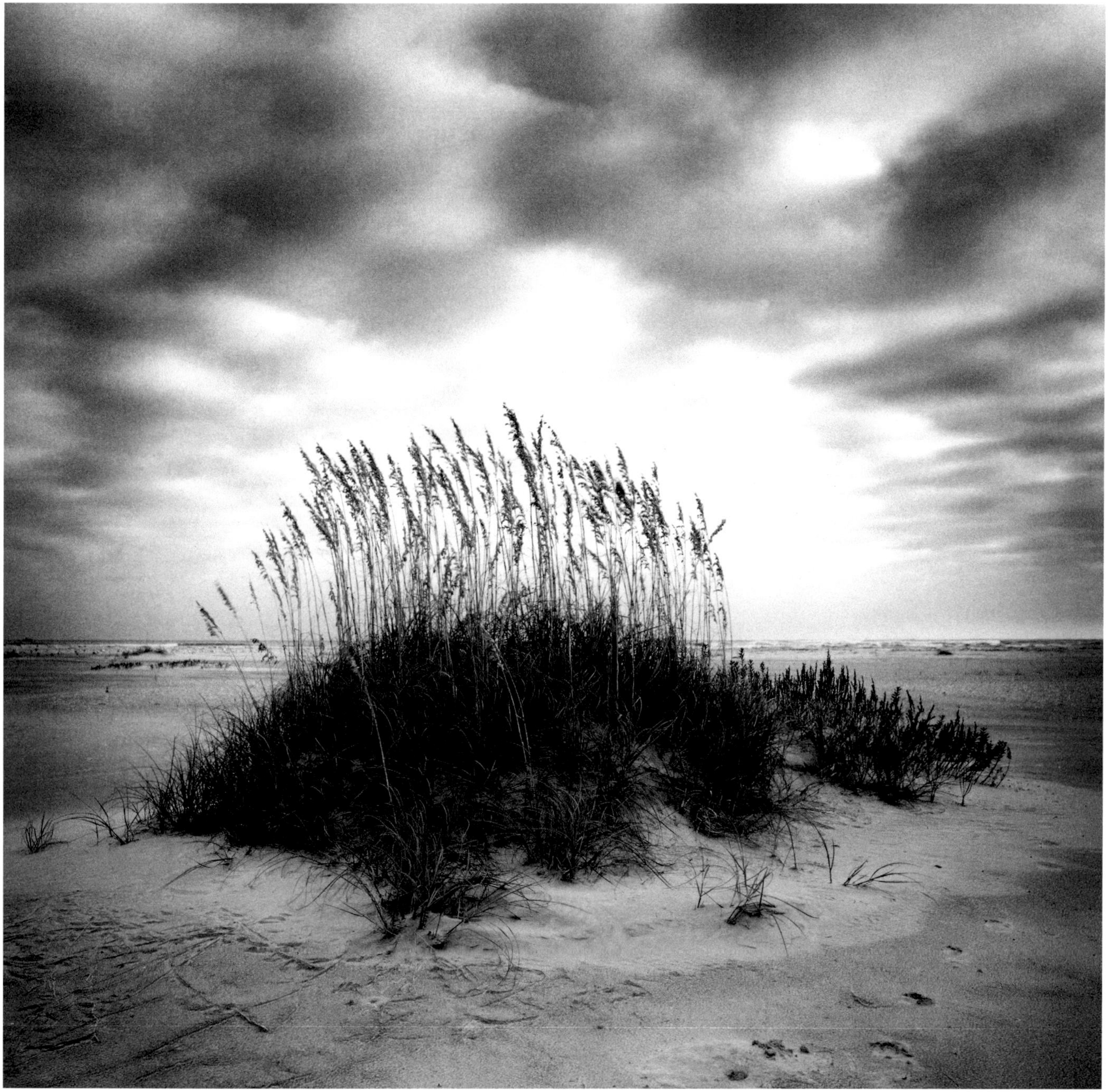

Atlantic Beachgrass, 2005

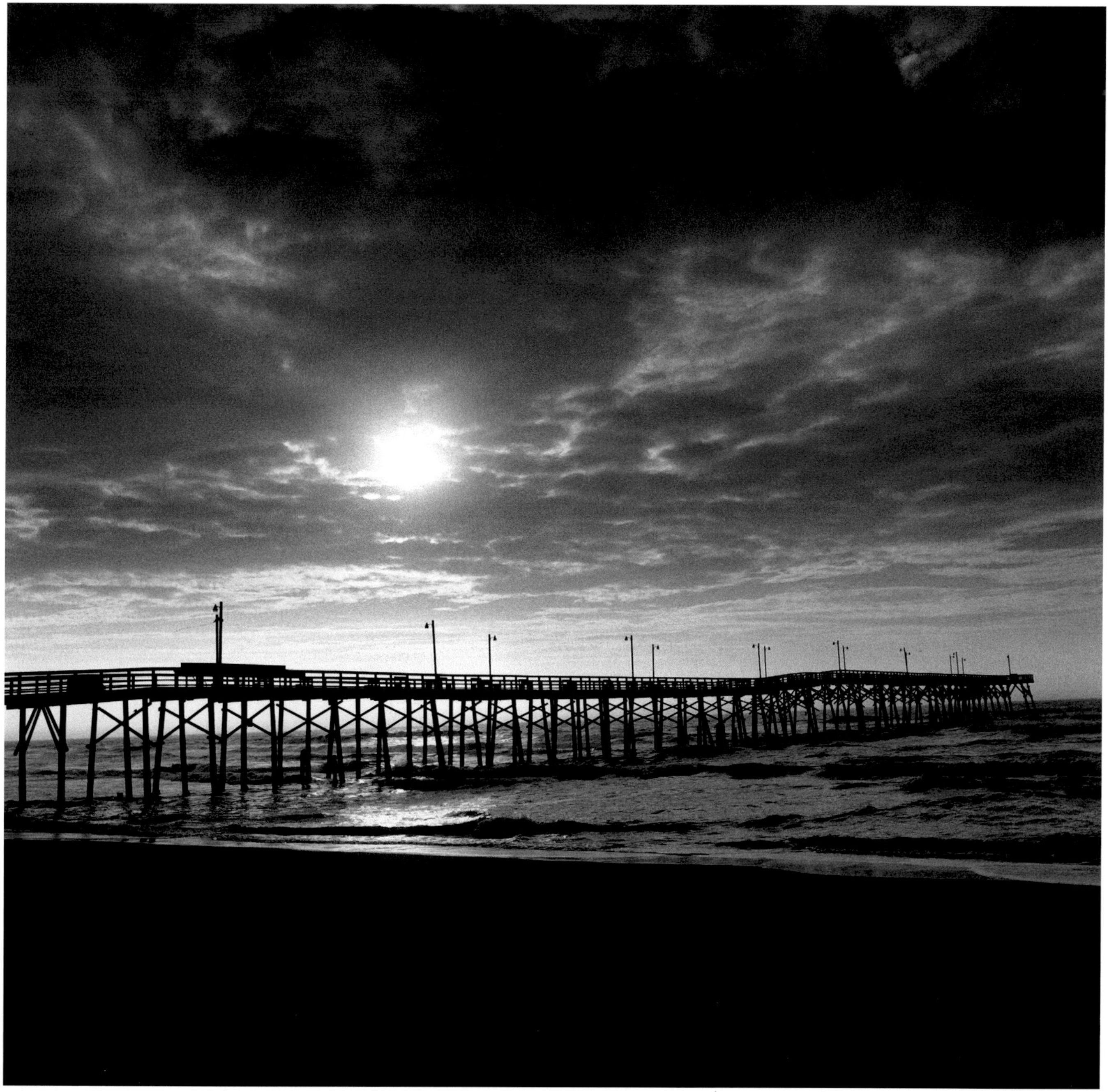

Fishing Pier, Topsail Beach, 2008

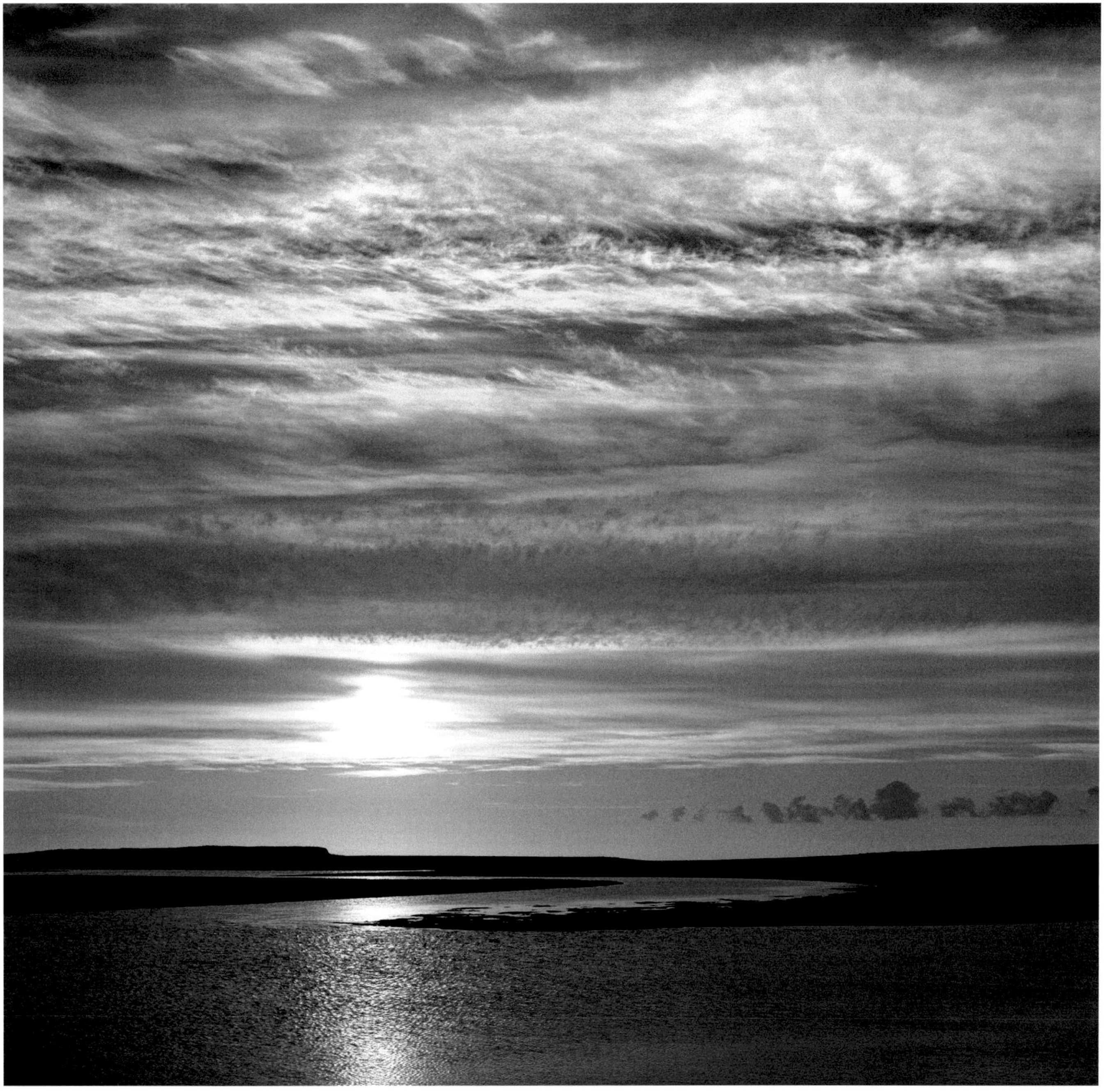

Layers, 2001

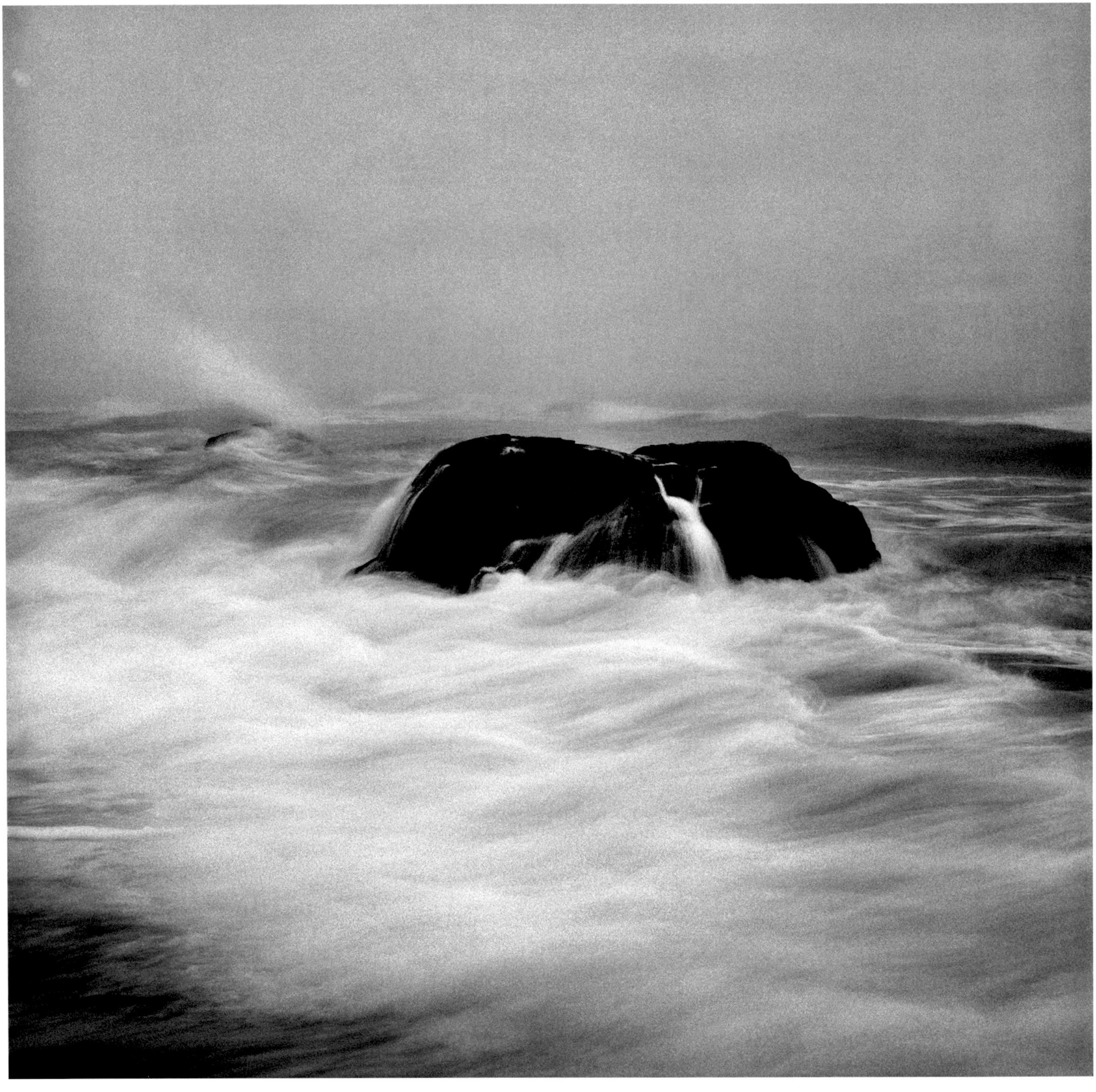

Lee Shore, 2004

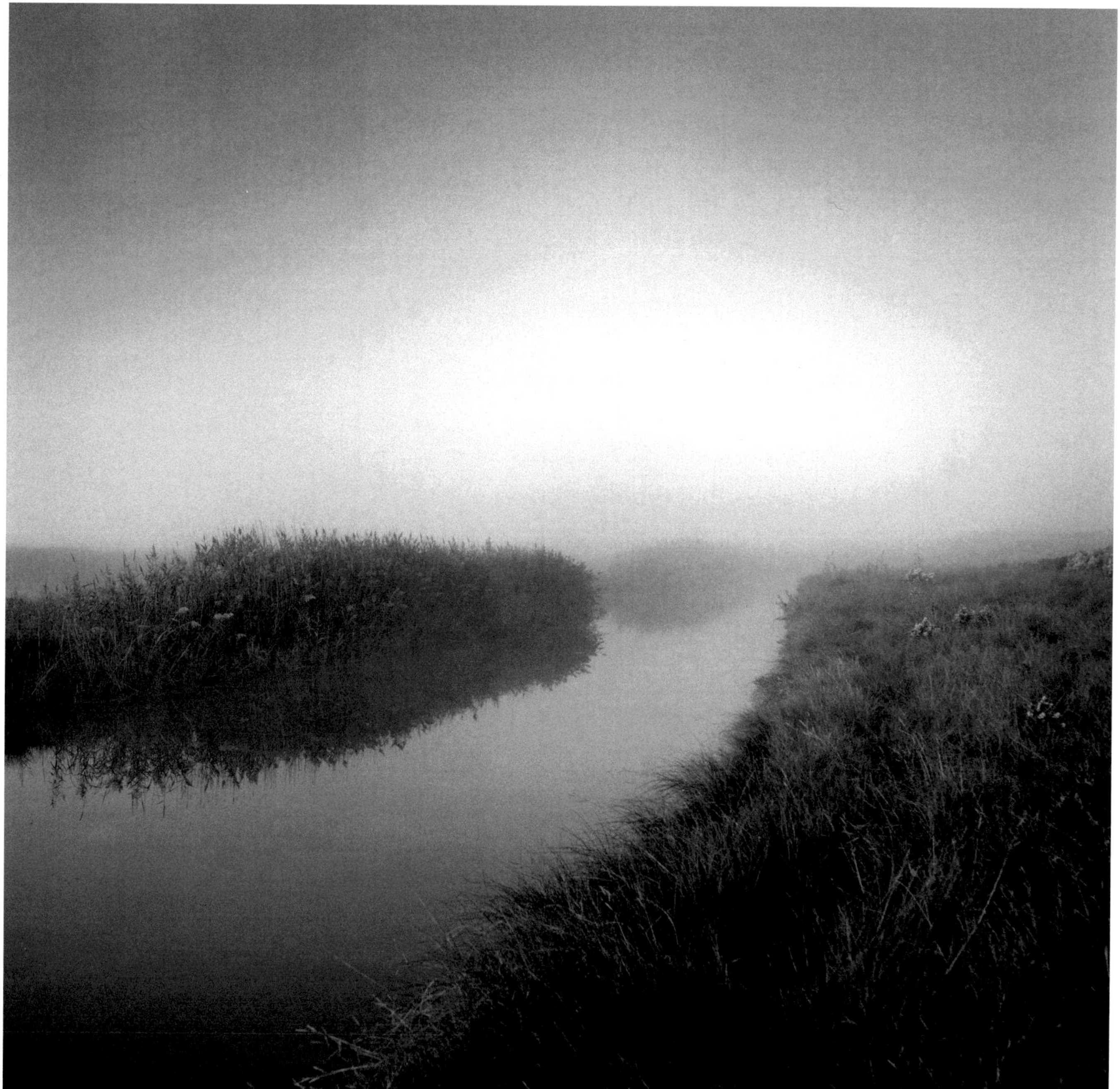

Quansoo in Fog, 2016

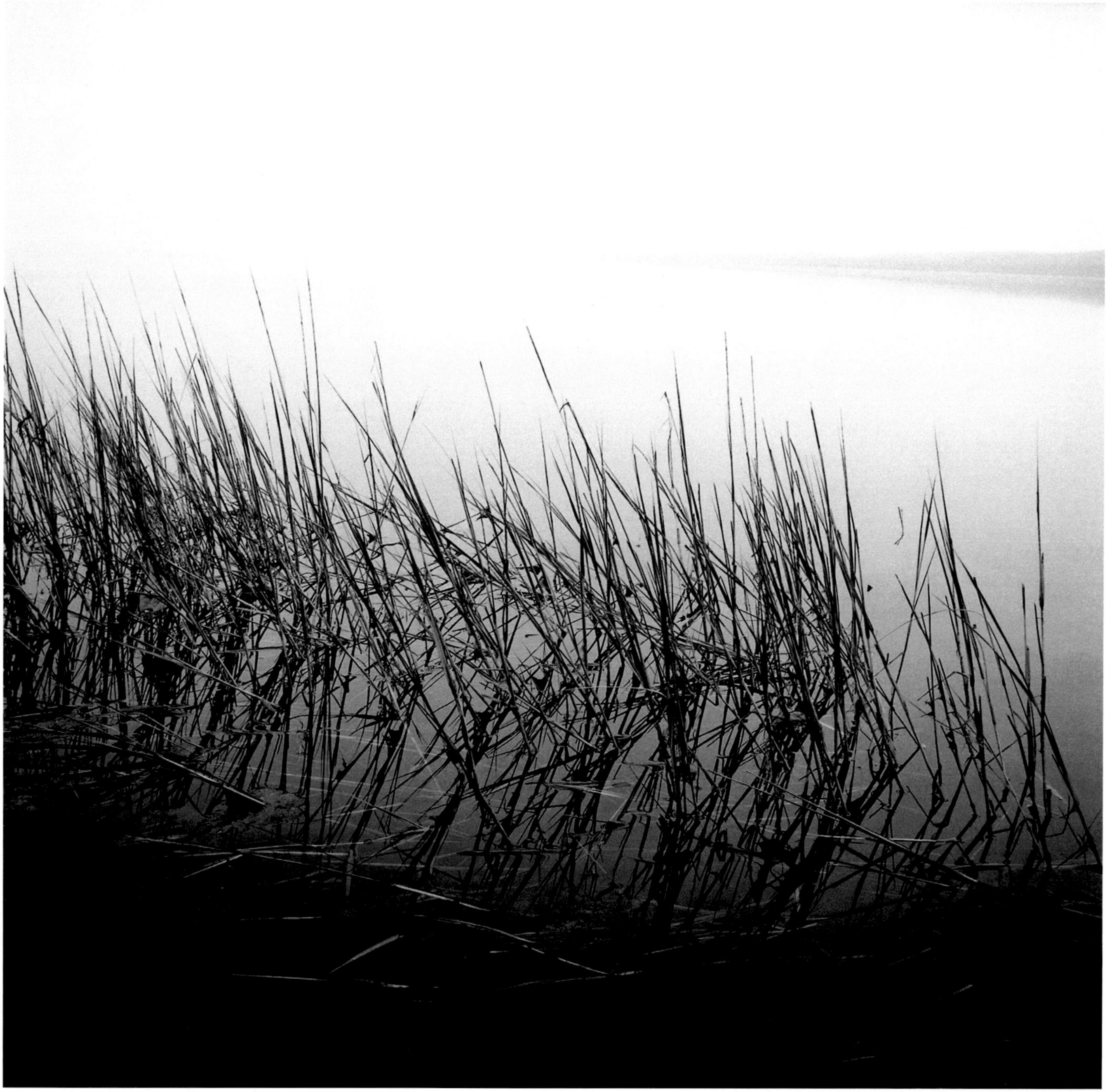

Reflections, 1999

Let the rhythm of the water set your soul free.

—CHRISTY ANN MARTINE

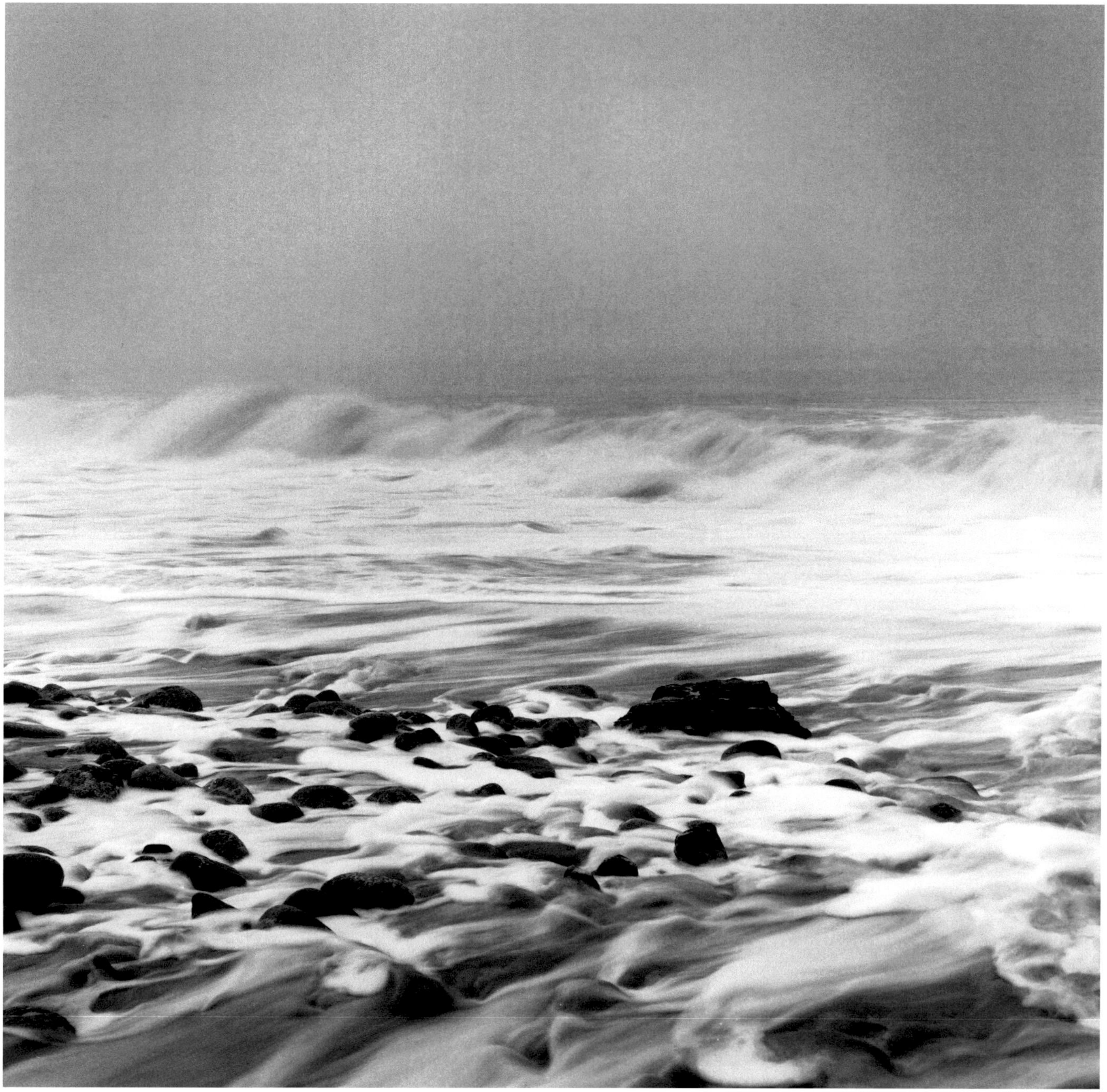

Veiled Surf, 2017

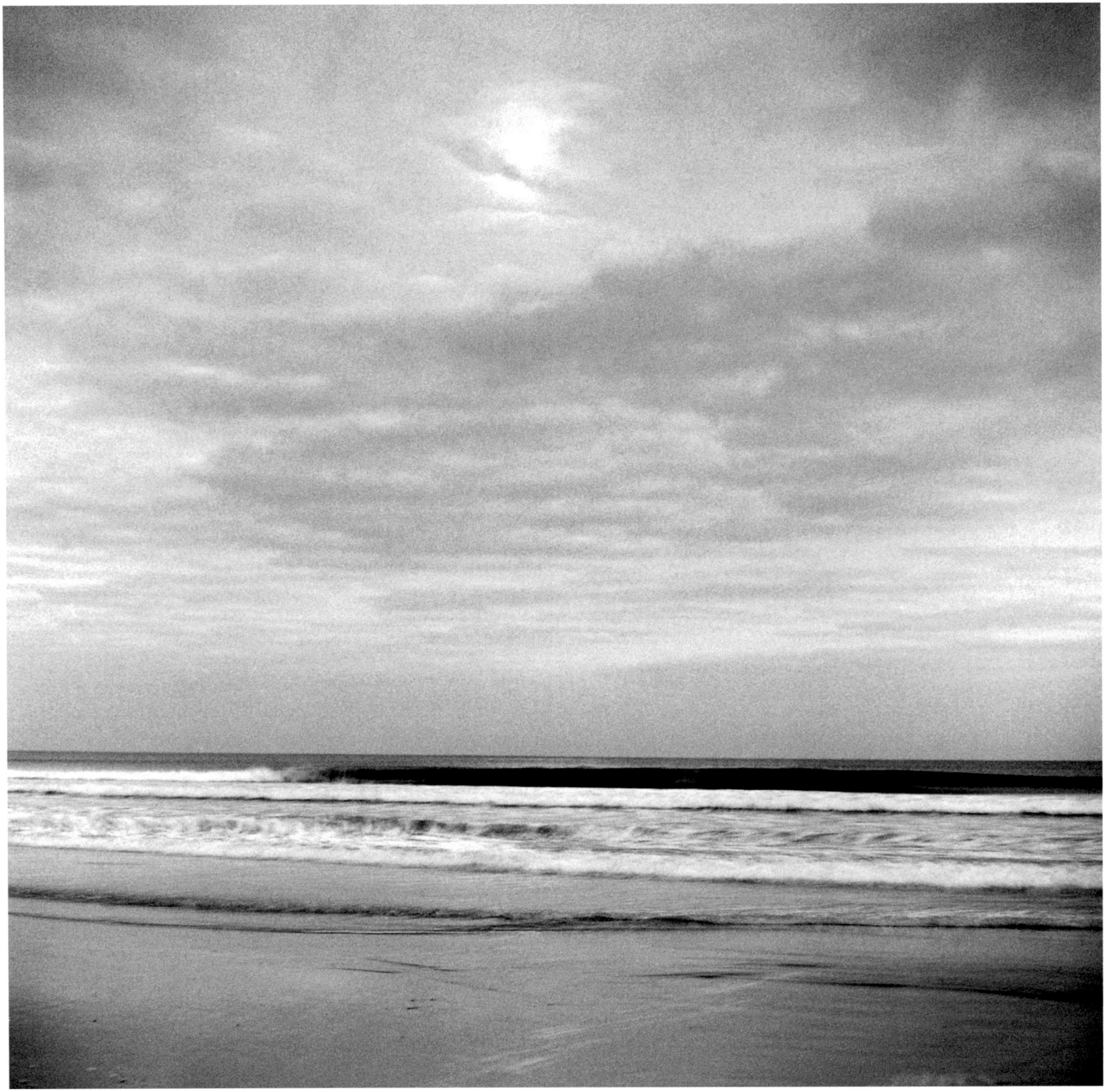

Silence, 2005

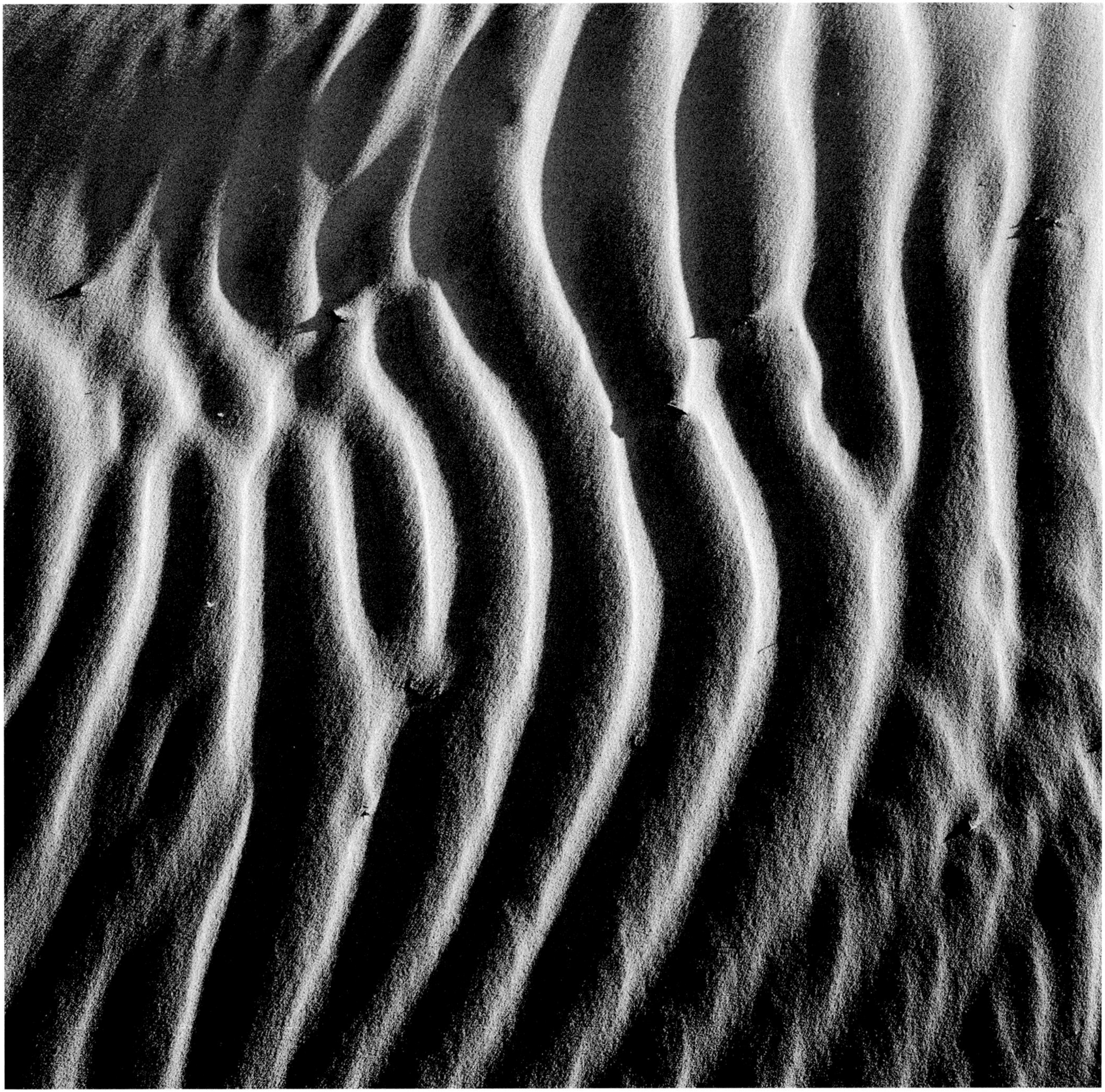

Sand Abstract, 2005

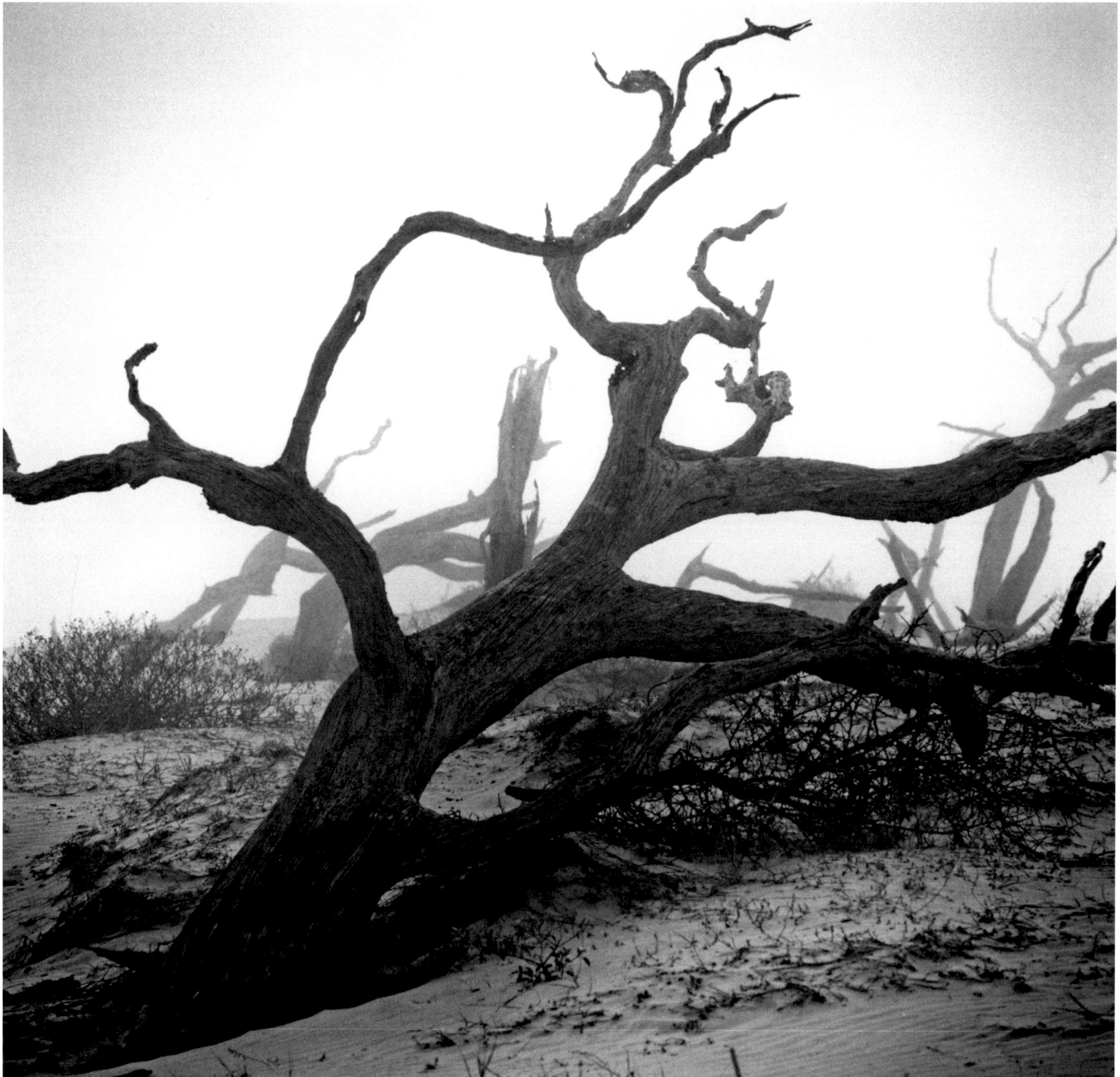

Twisted Oaks, Georgia, 2001

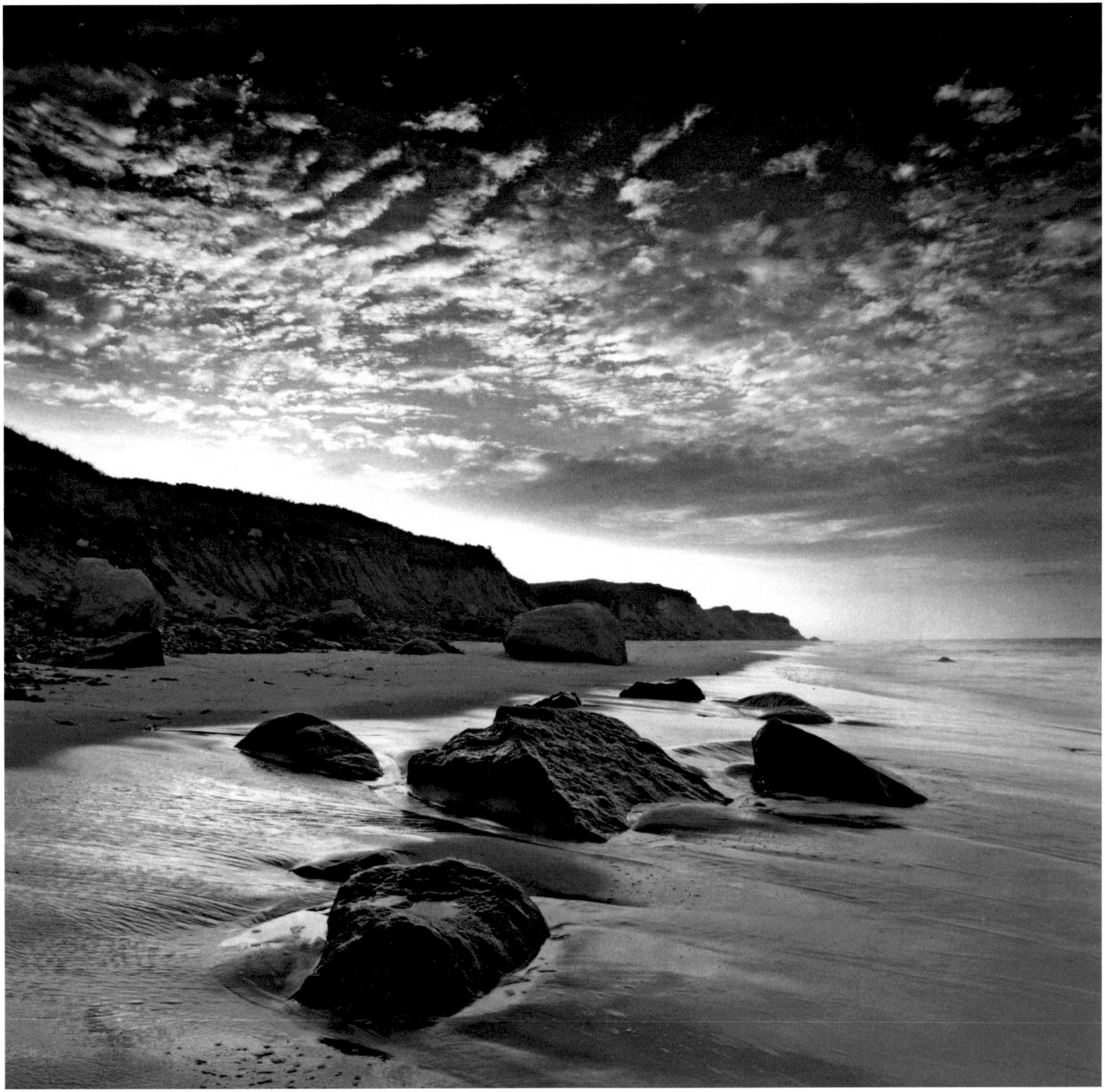

Zack's Cliffs, 2015

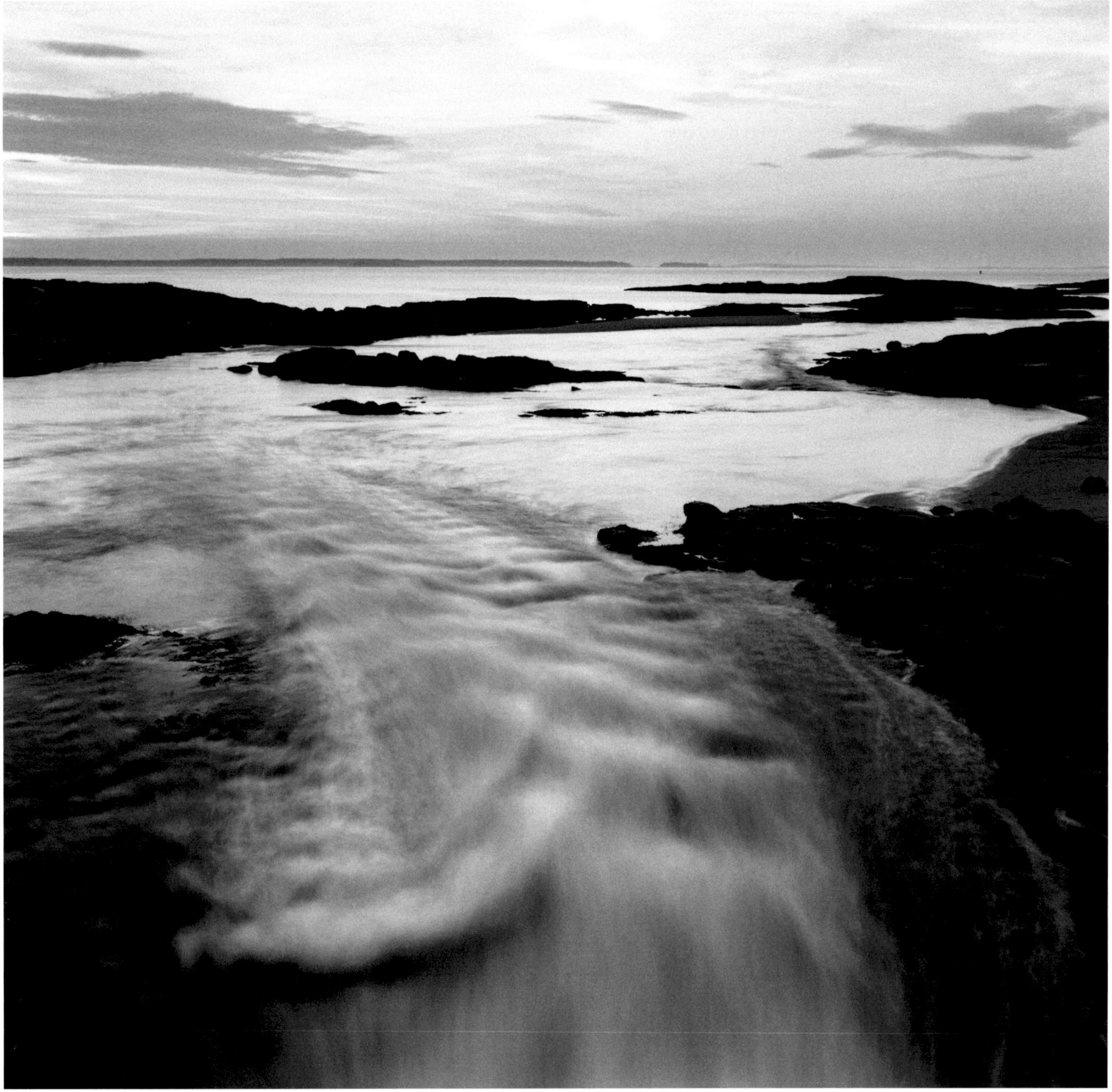

Returning, *Reid State Park*, 2002

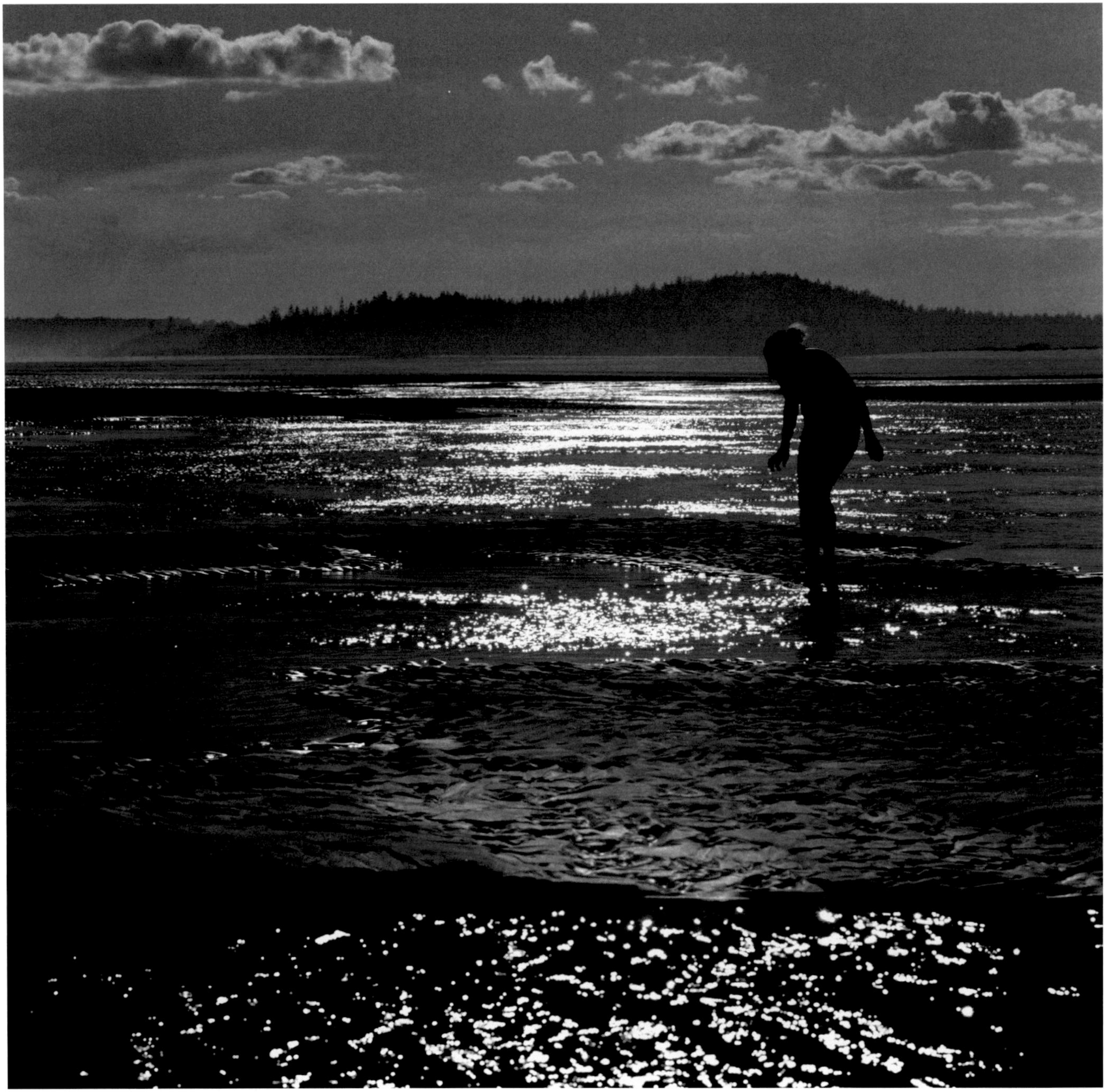

Searching for Something, 2011

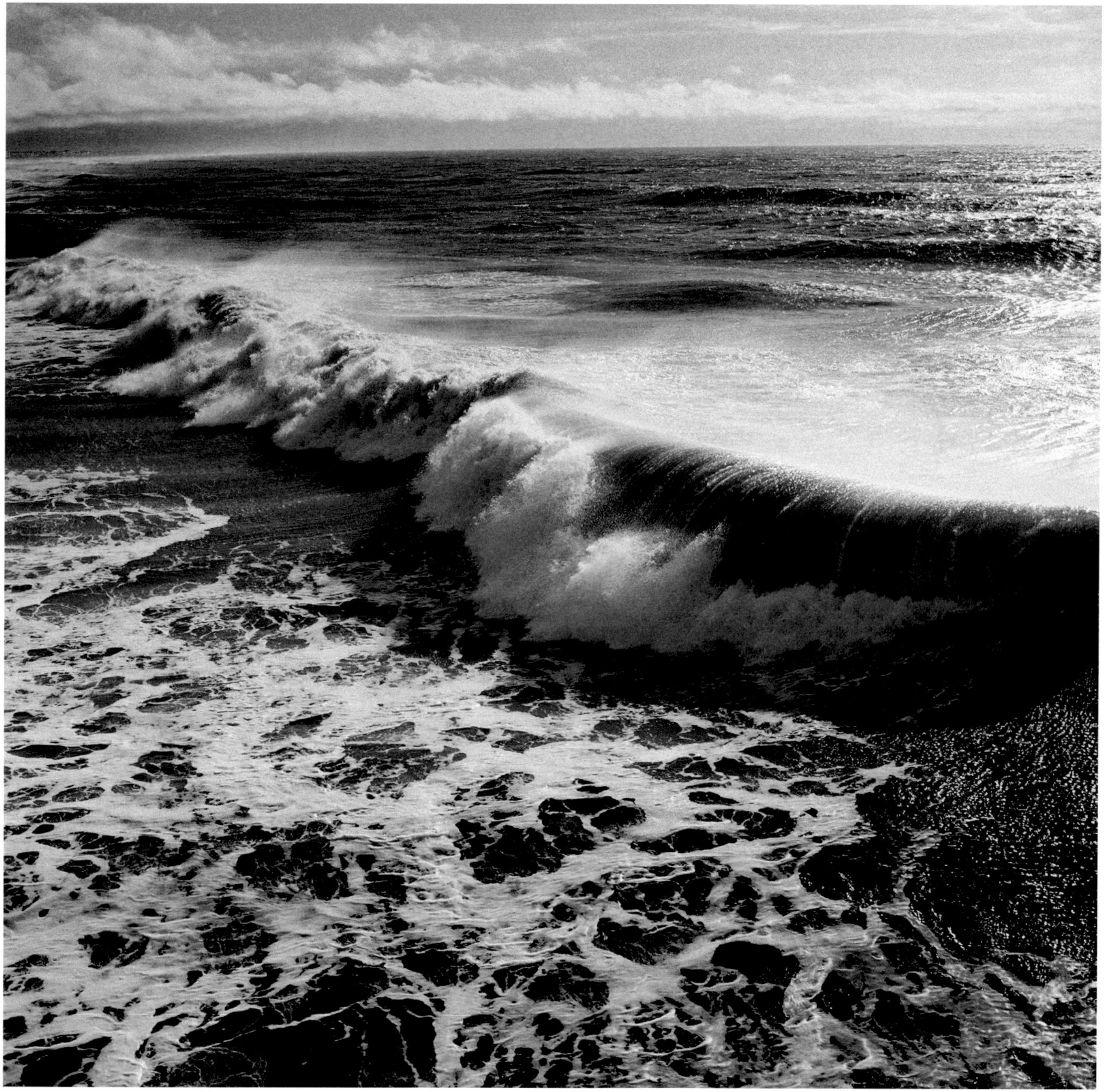

Wave Study, 2007

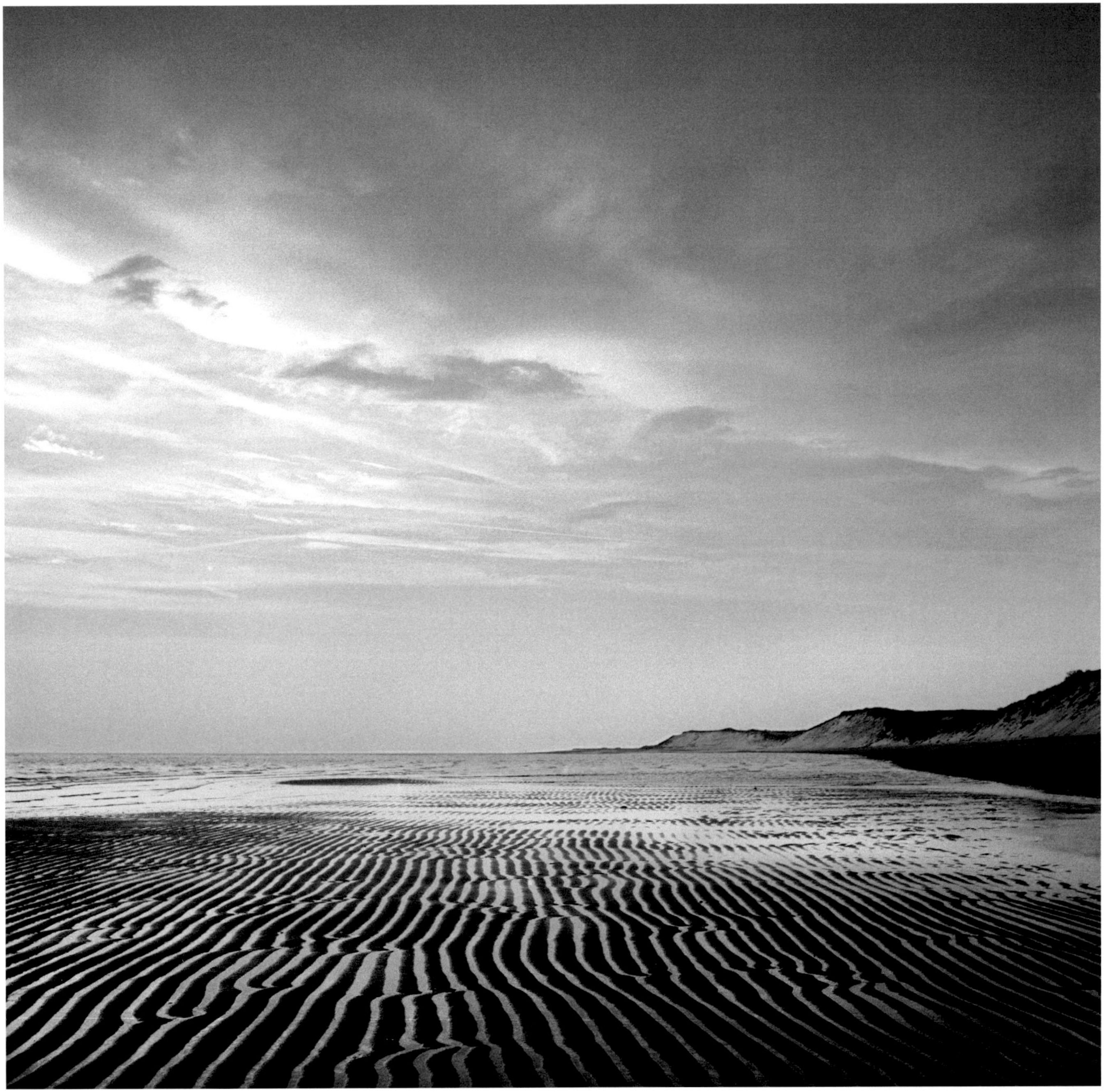

Wellfleet Flats, 2003

All that we do
Is touched with ocean, yet we remain
On the shore of what we know.

—RICHARD WILBUR

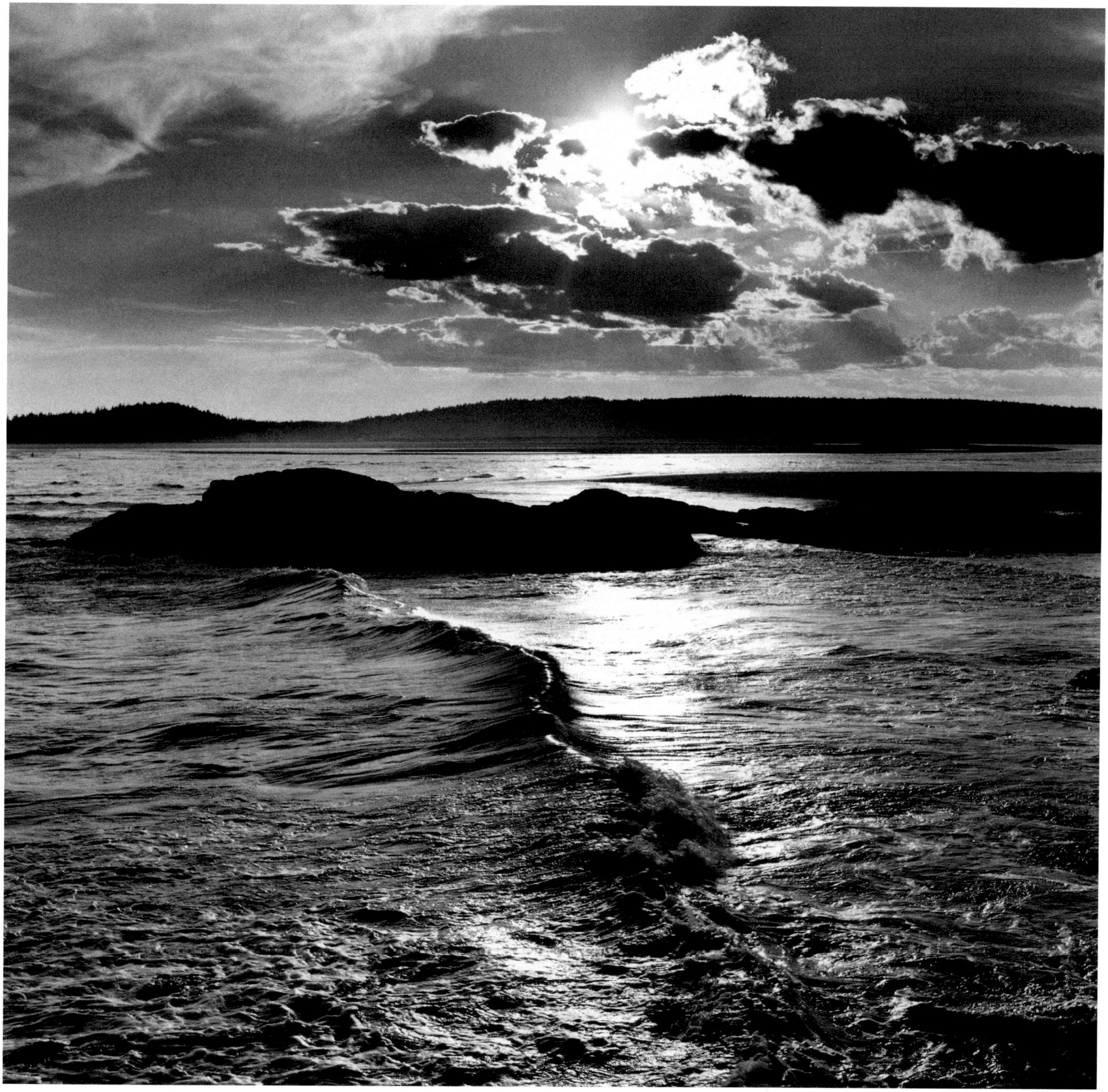

North Shore, 2006

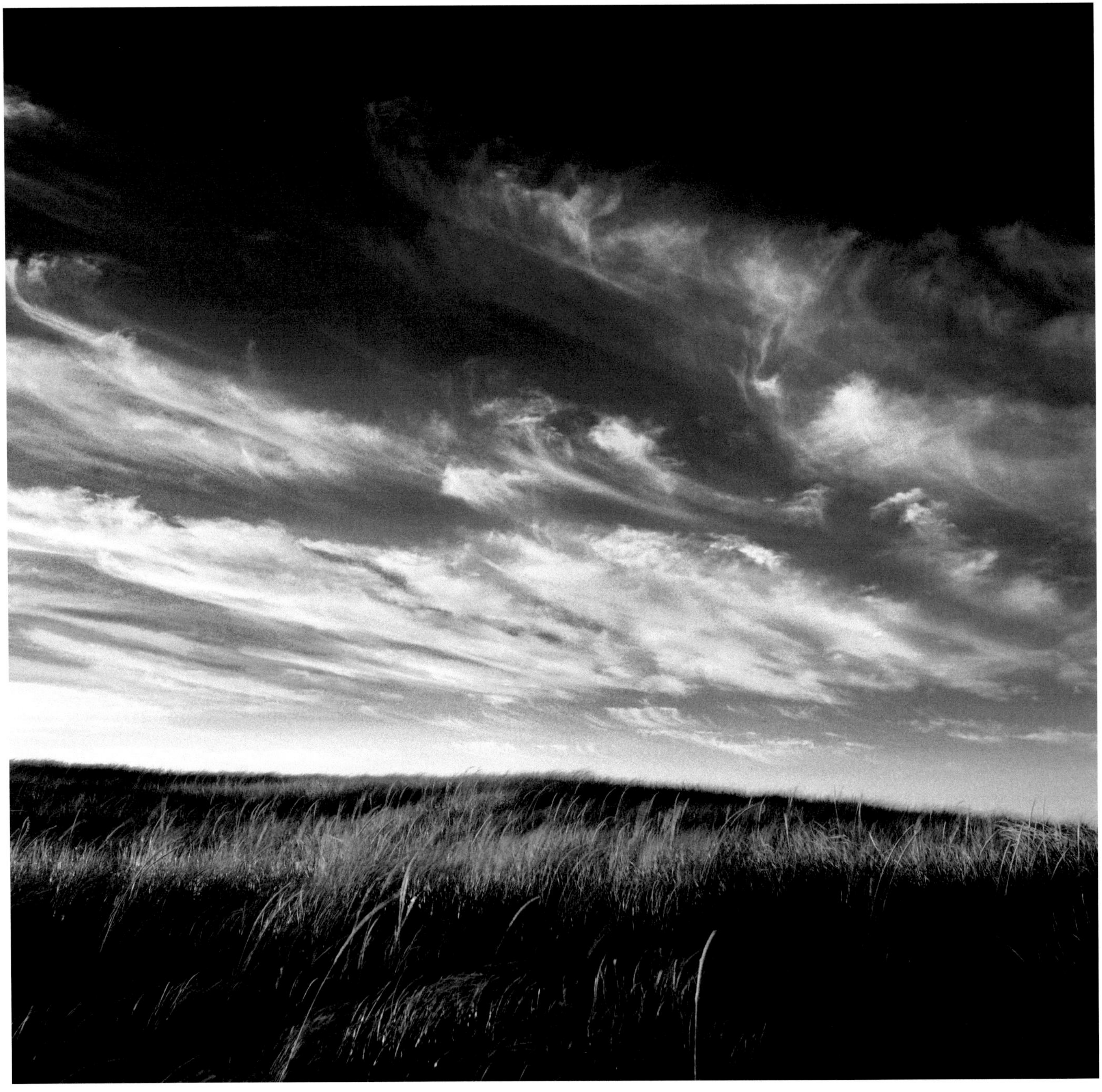

Nantucket Winds, 2005

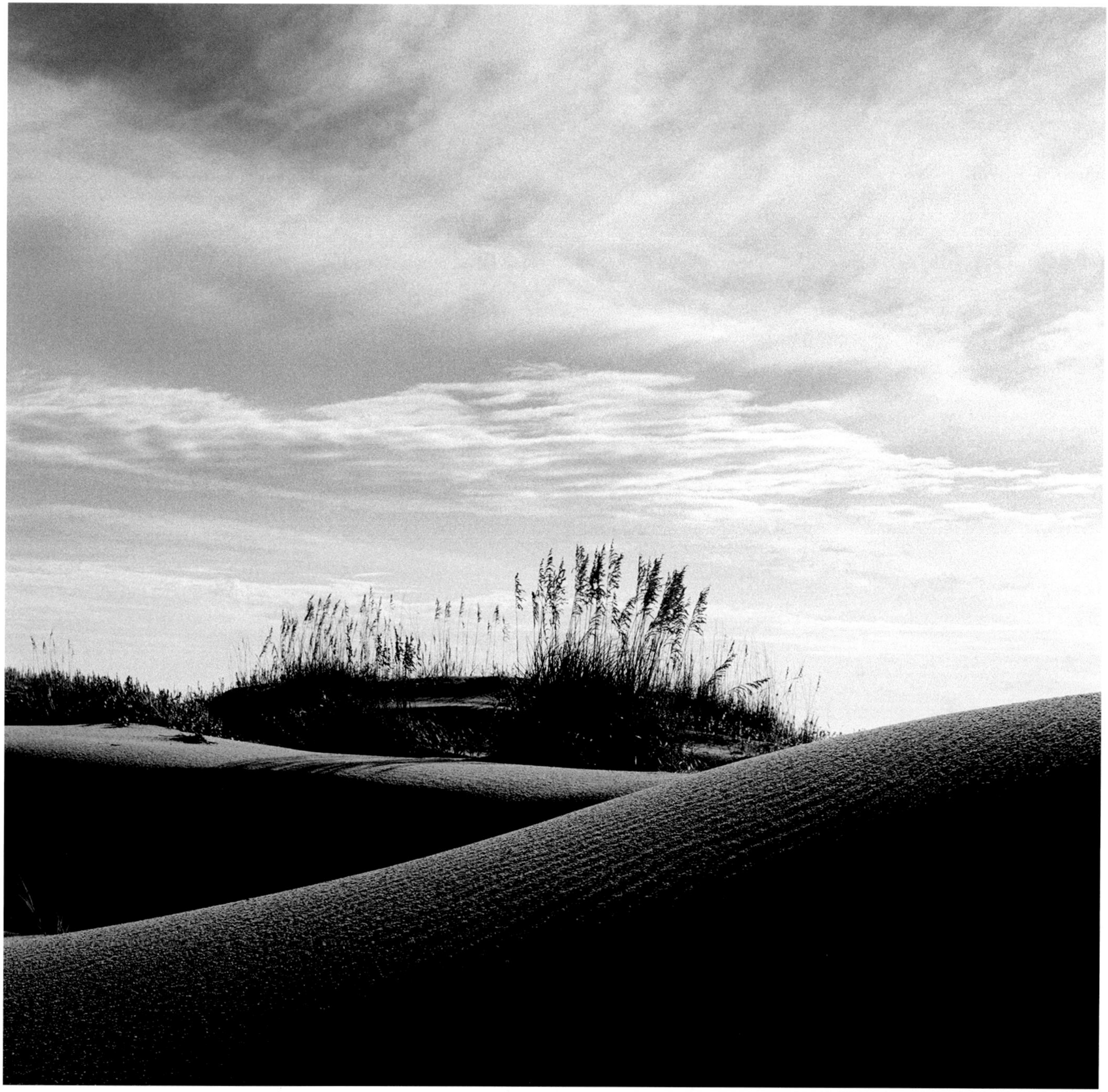

Atlantic Dunes, 2006

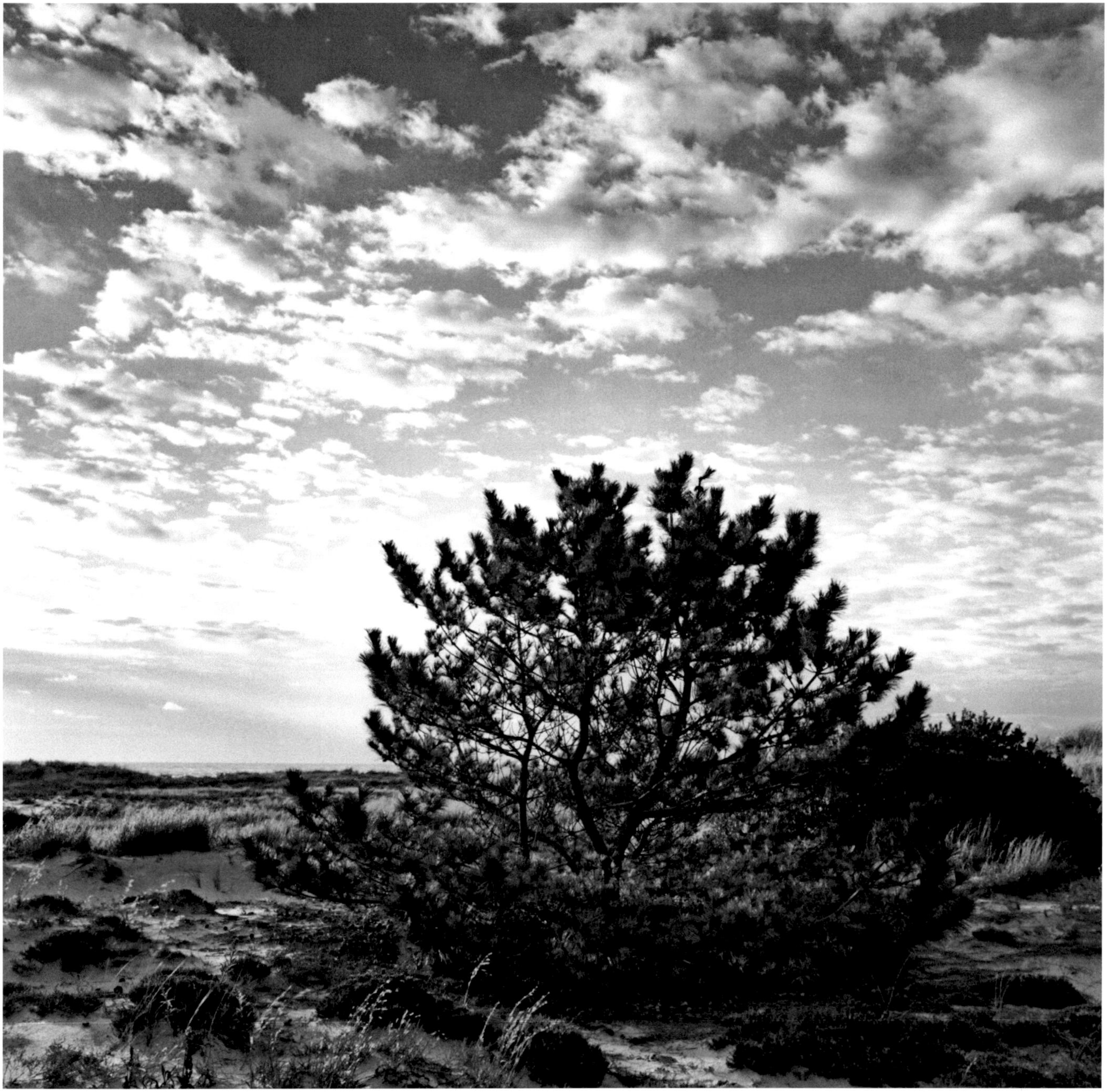

Scrub Pine, 2017

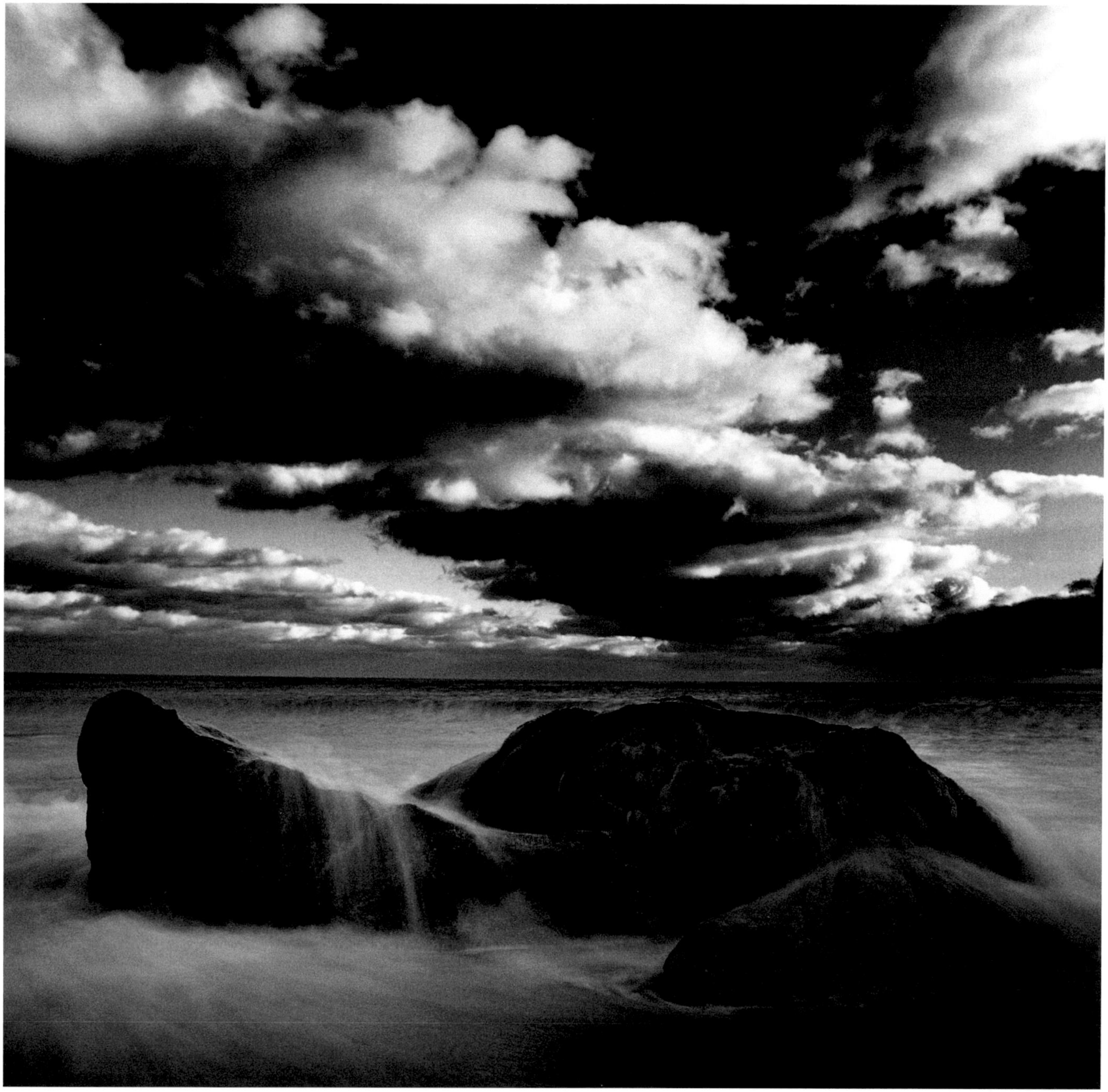

Rising Tide, 1999

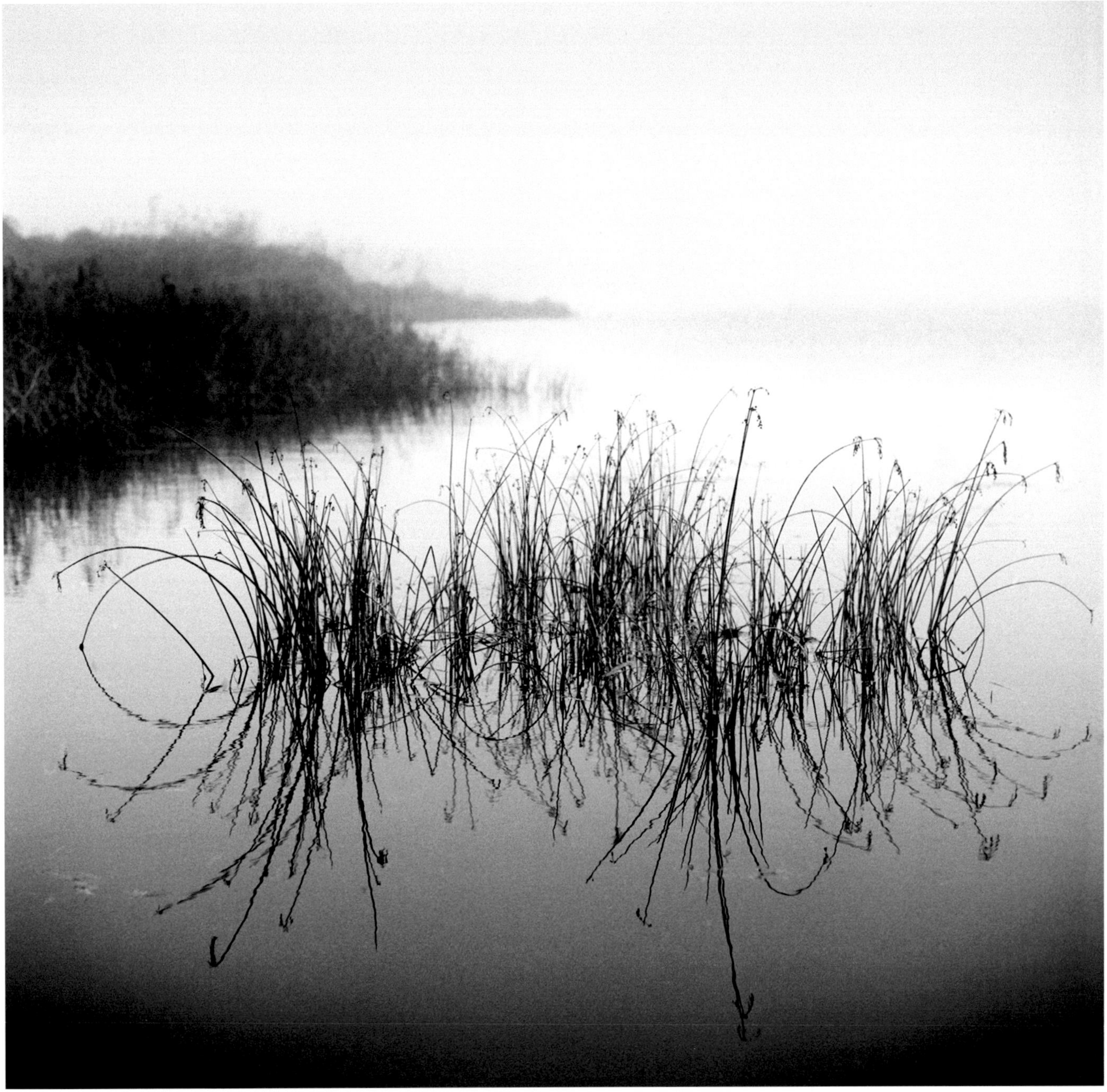

Reeds, 2004

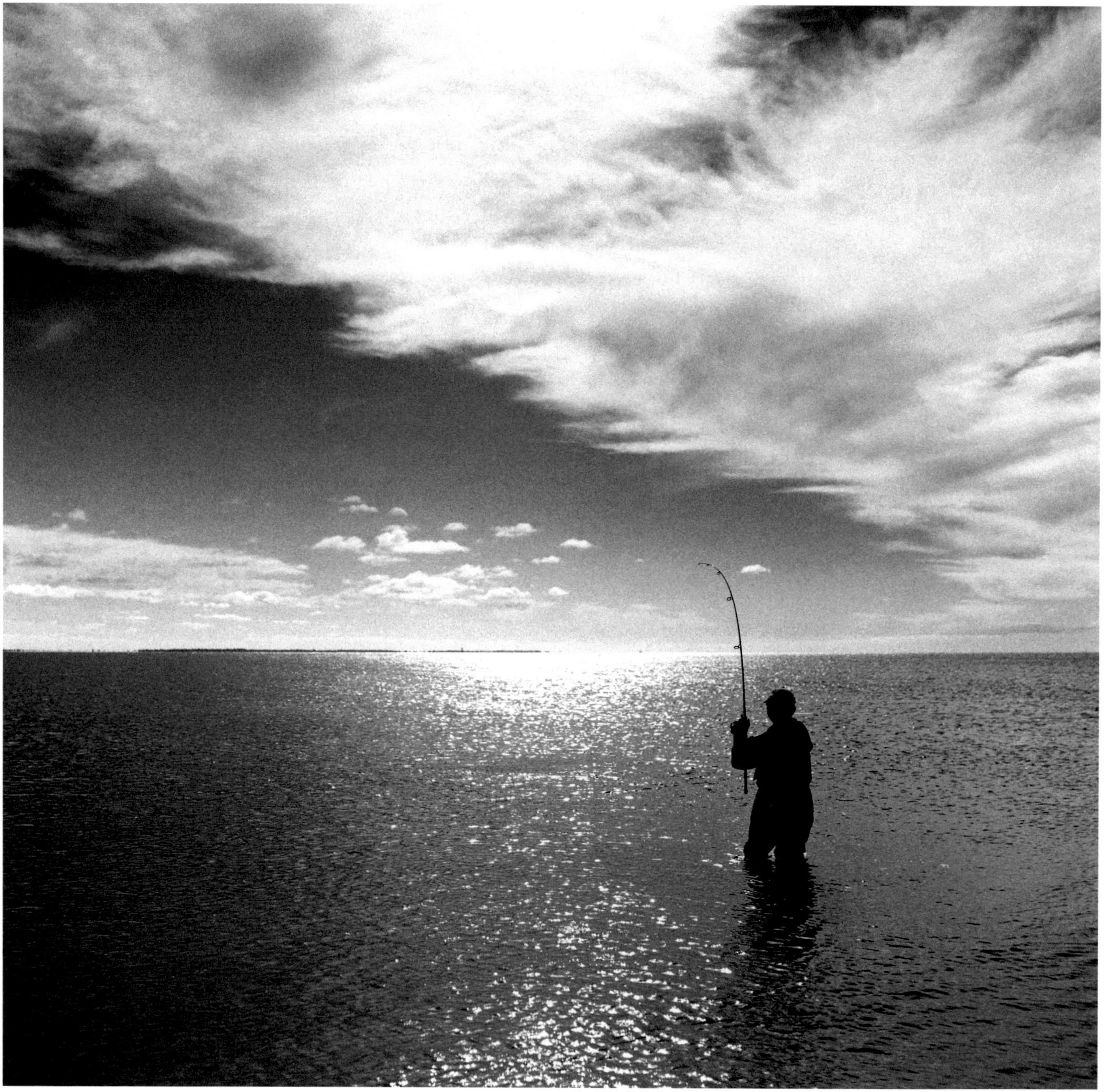

Fisherman, 2005

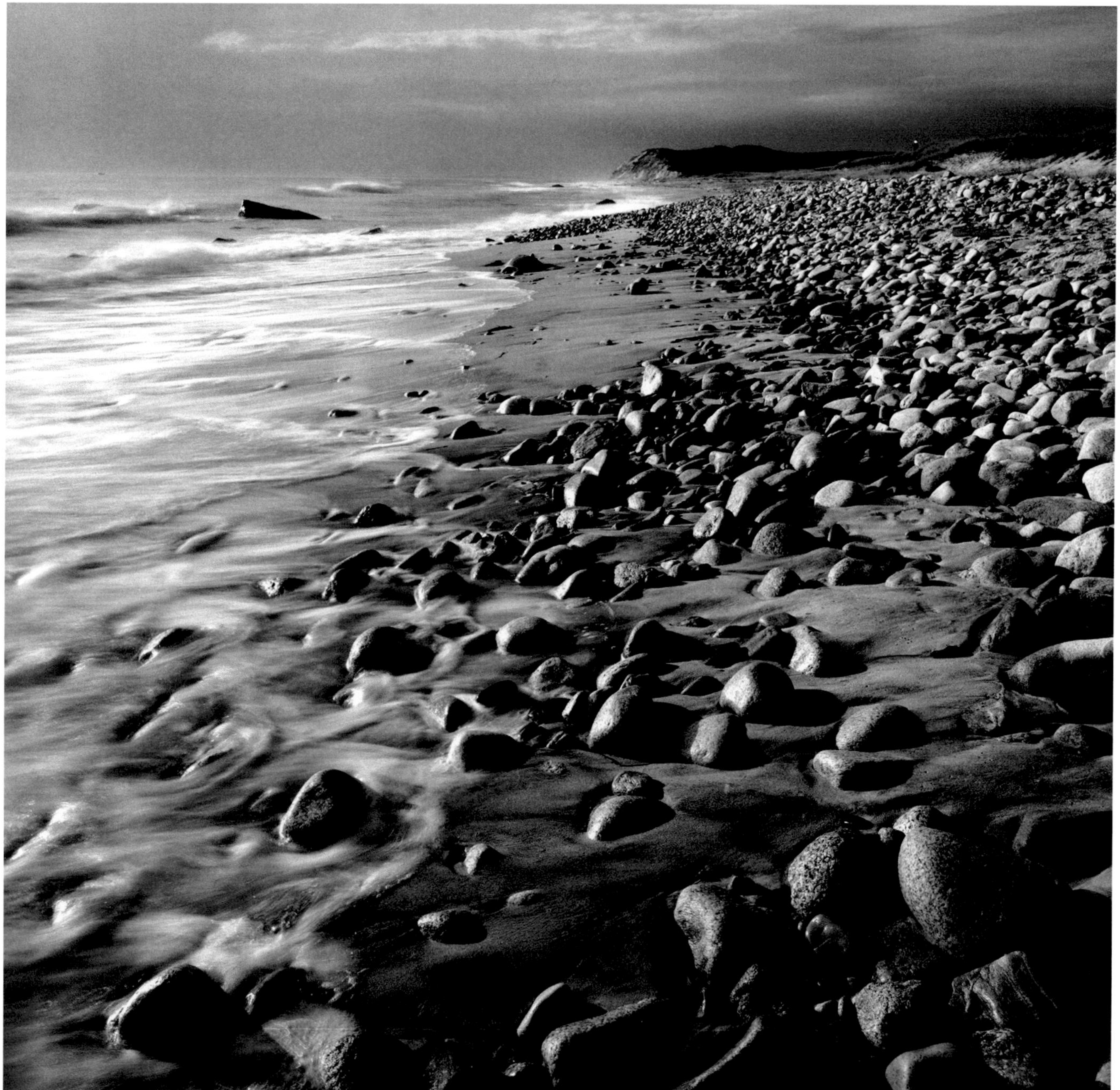

Philbin Beach, 1998

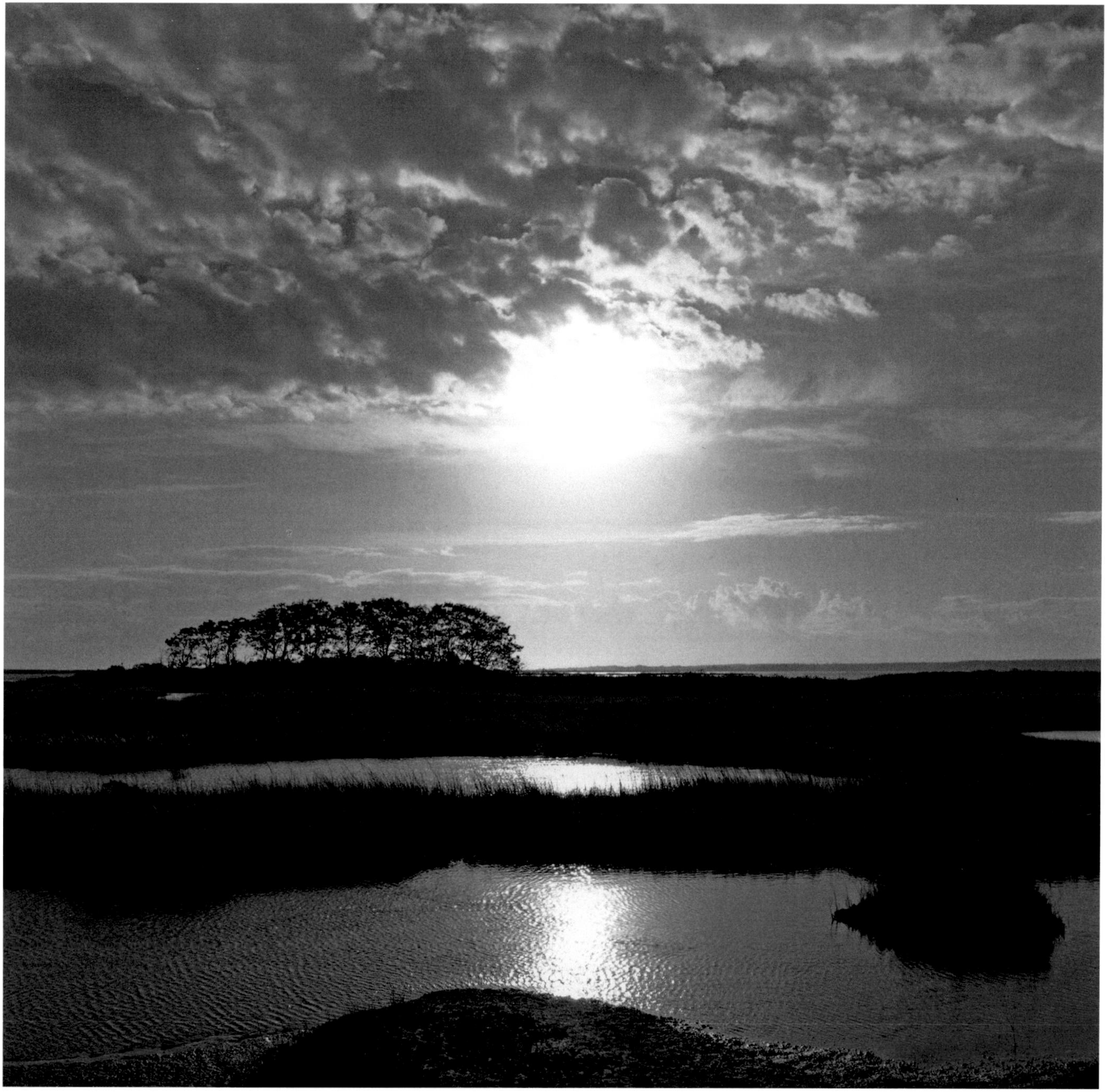

Long Point, 2012

Surely the sea
is the most beautiful fact
in our universe . . .

—MARY OLIVER

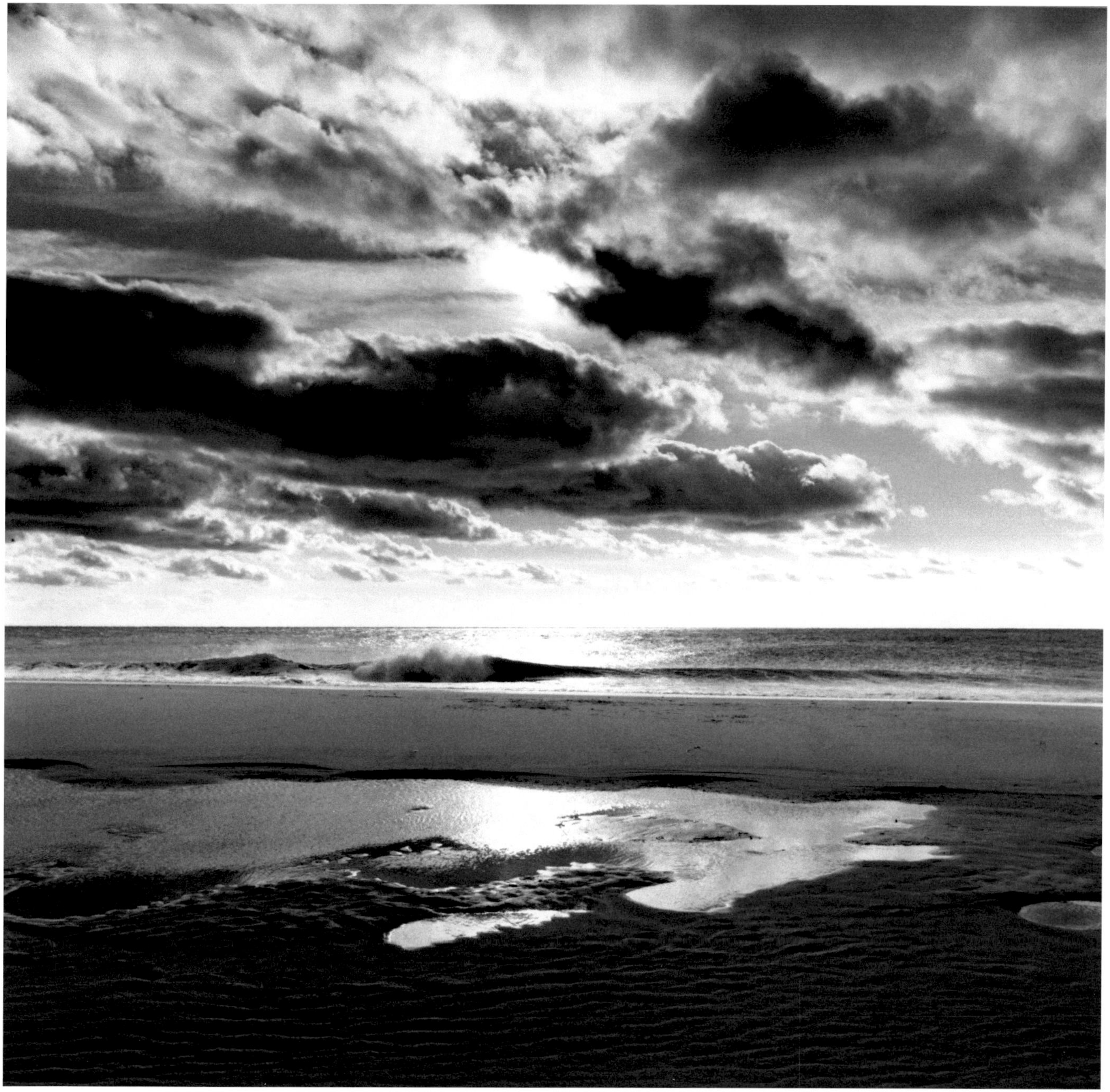

Peaceful Moment, 2017

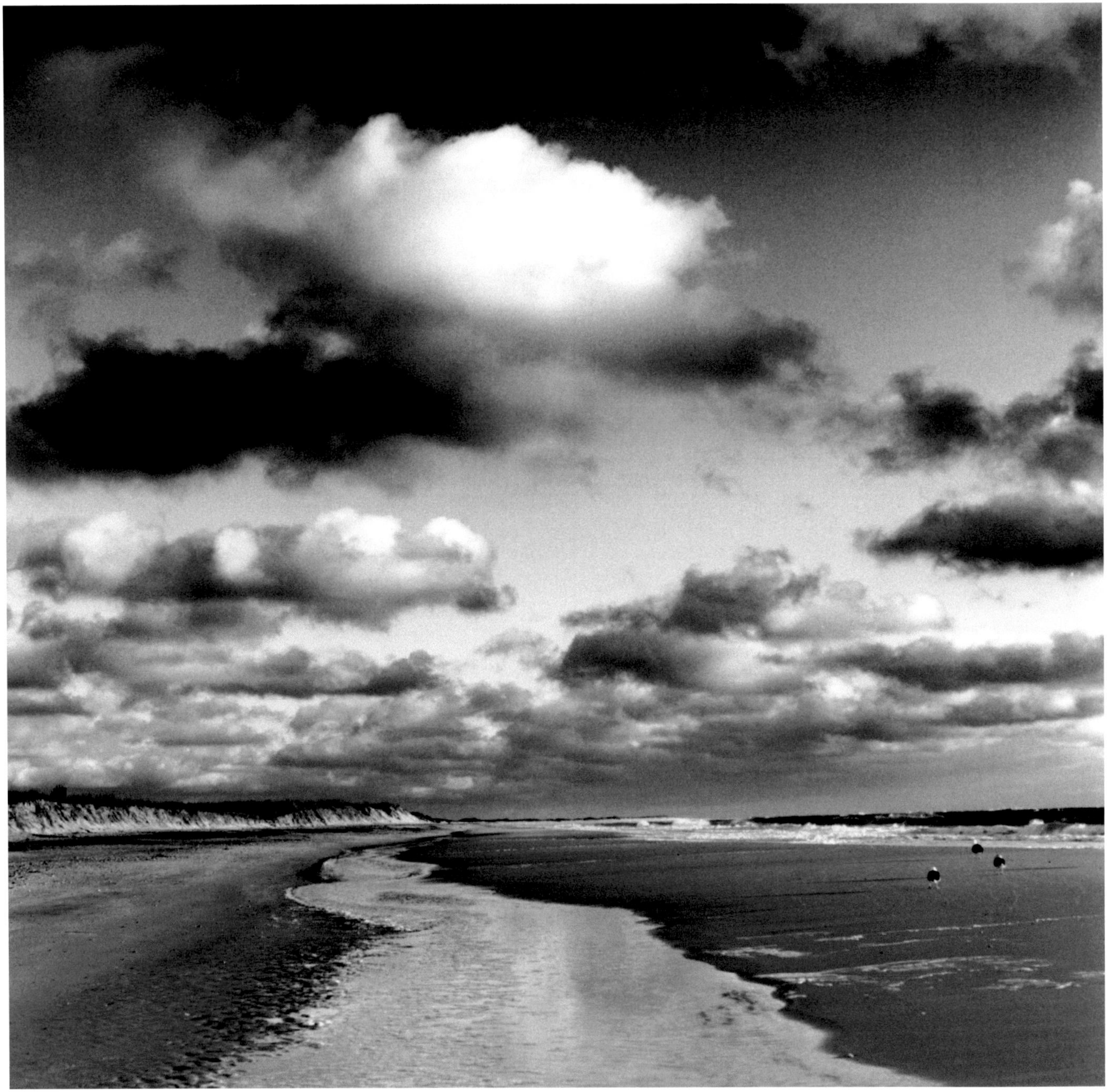

Seagulls, Barnegat Light, 2017

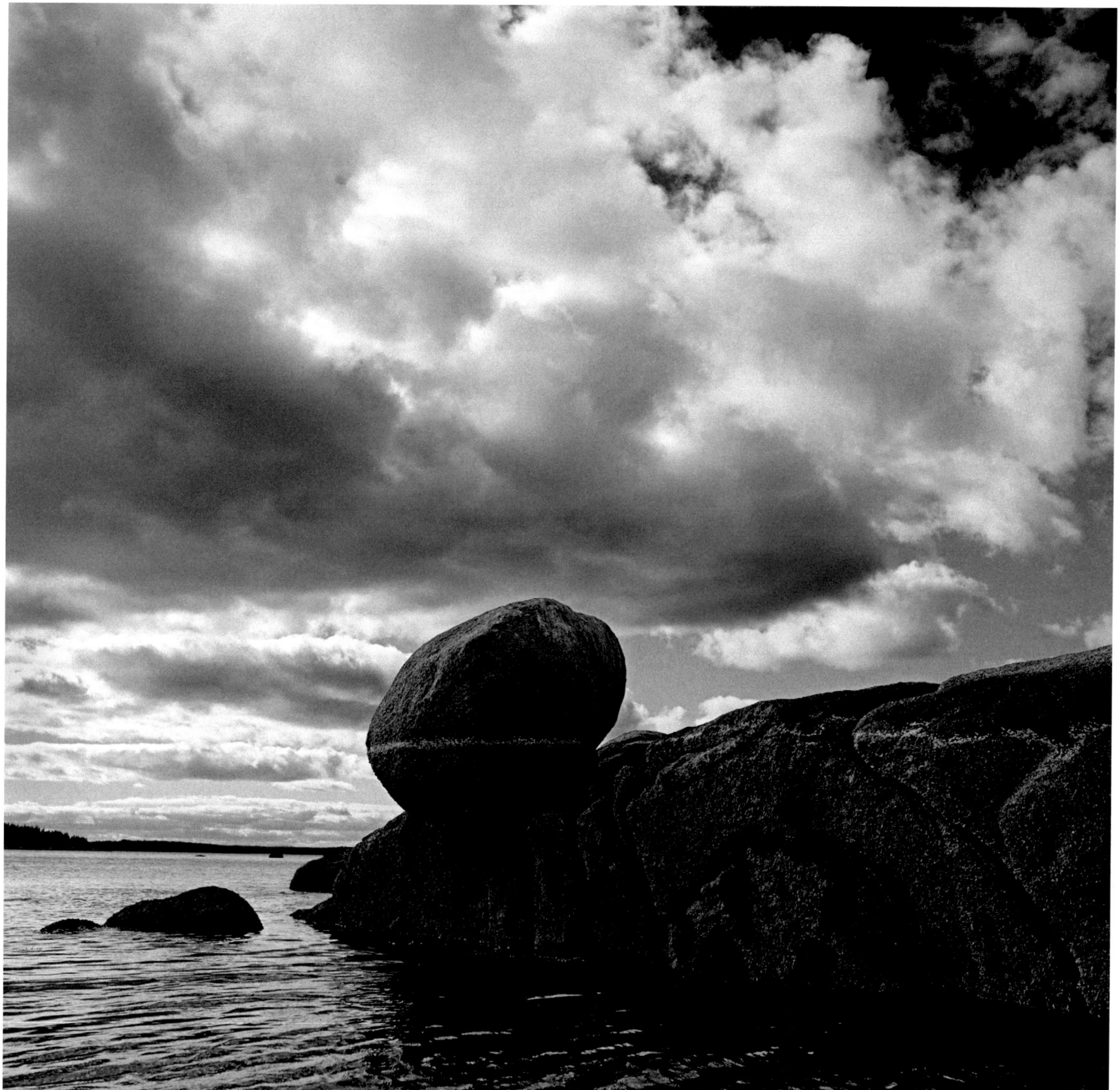

Glacial Erratic, 2010

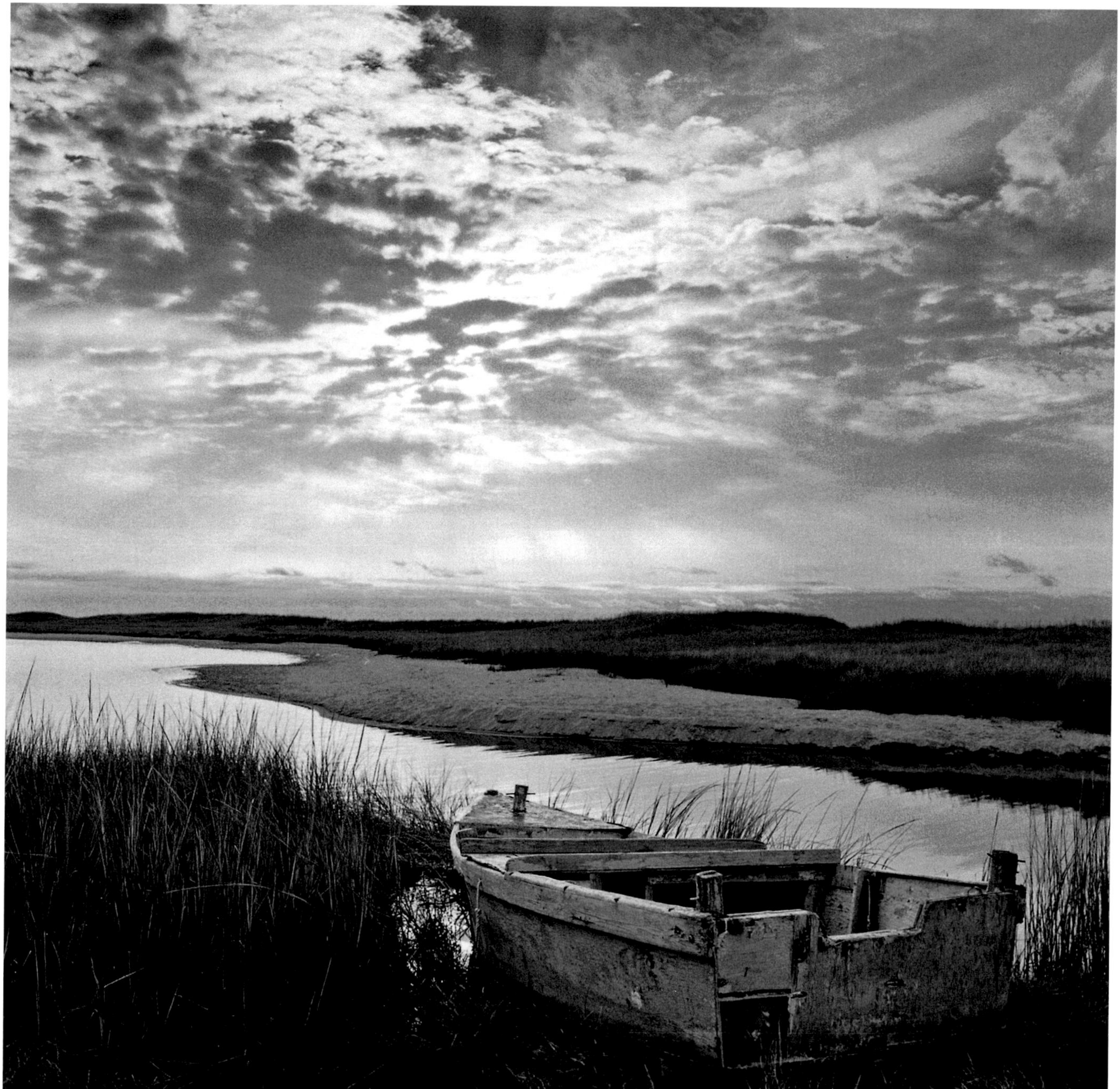

Old Oyster Boat, 2000

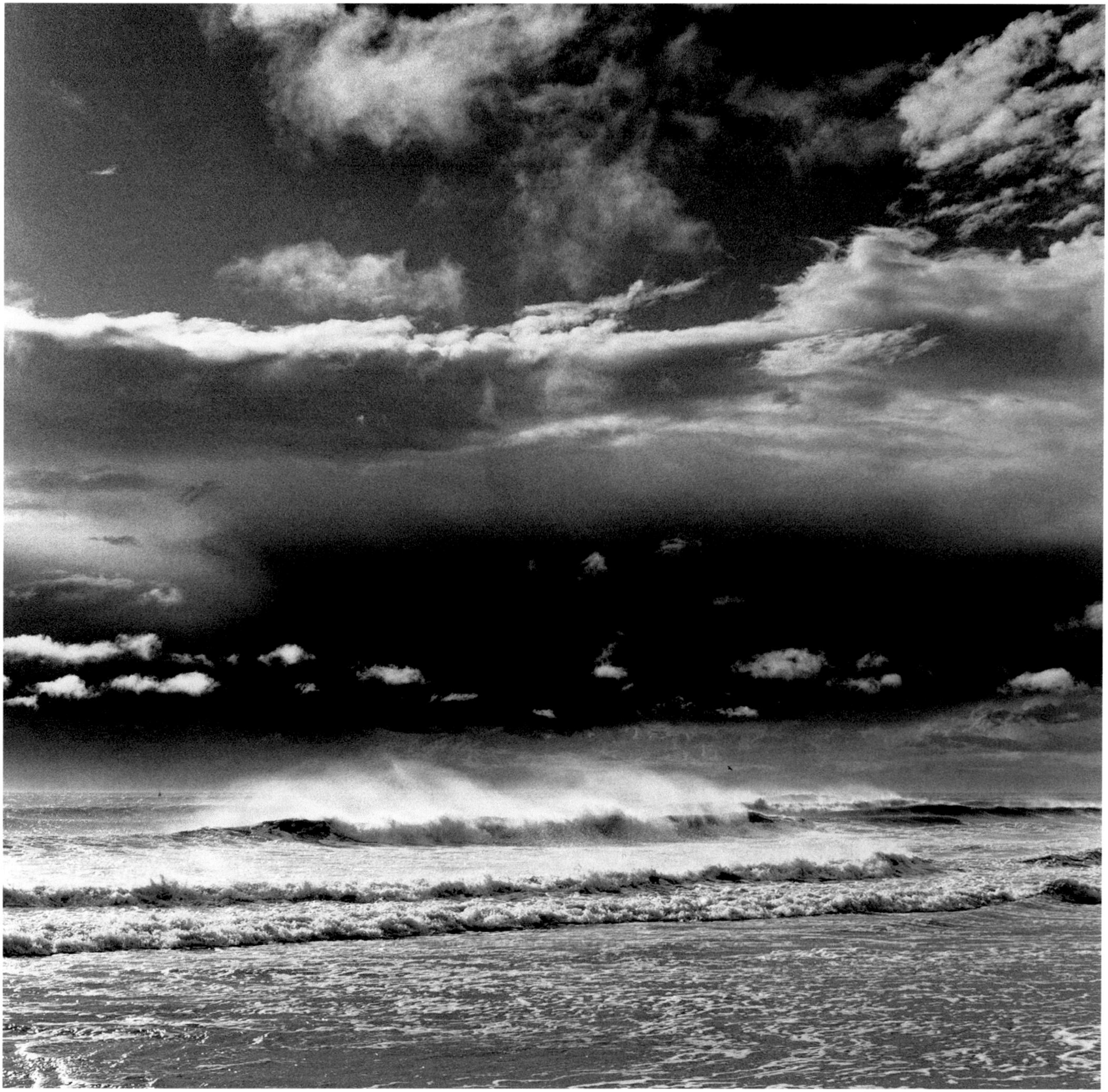

Wind Swept, 2006

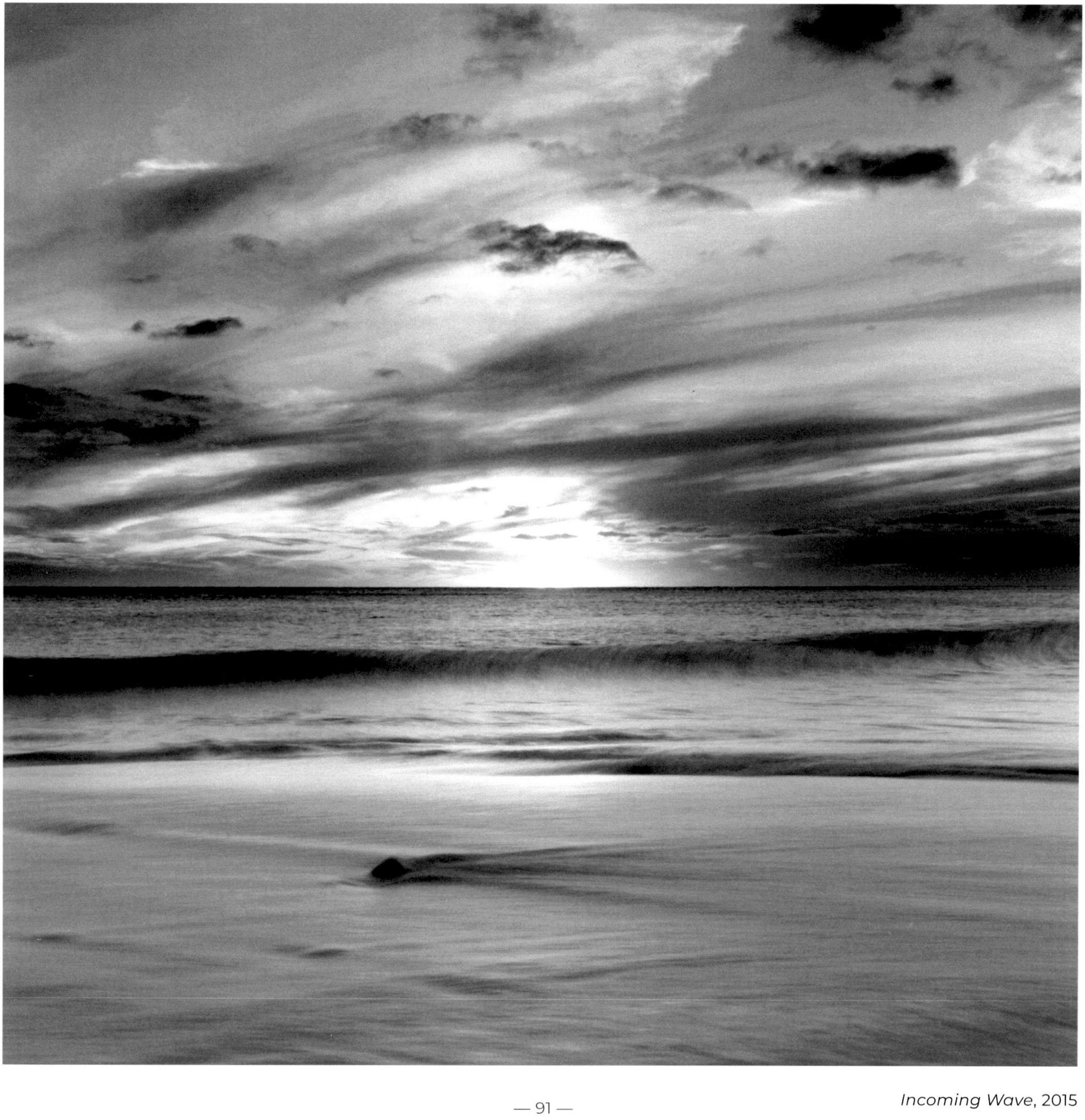

Incoming Wave, 2015

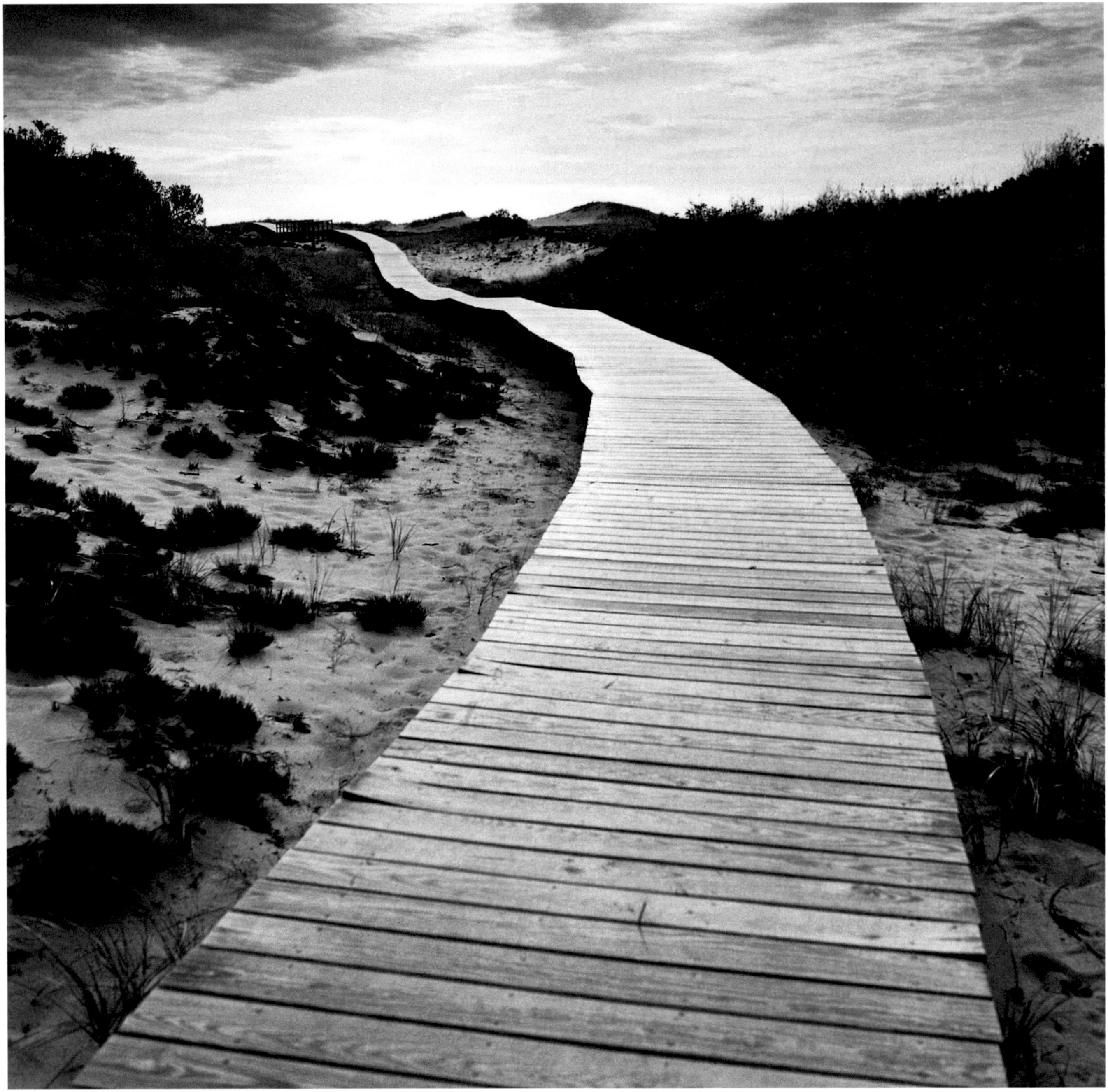

Dune Boardwalk, 2002

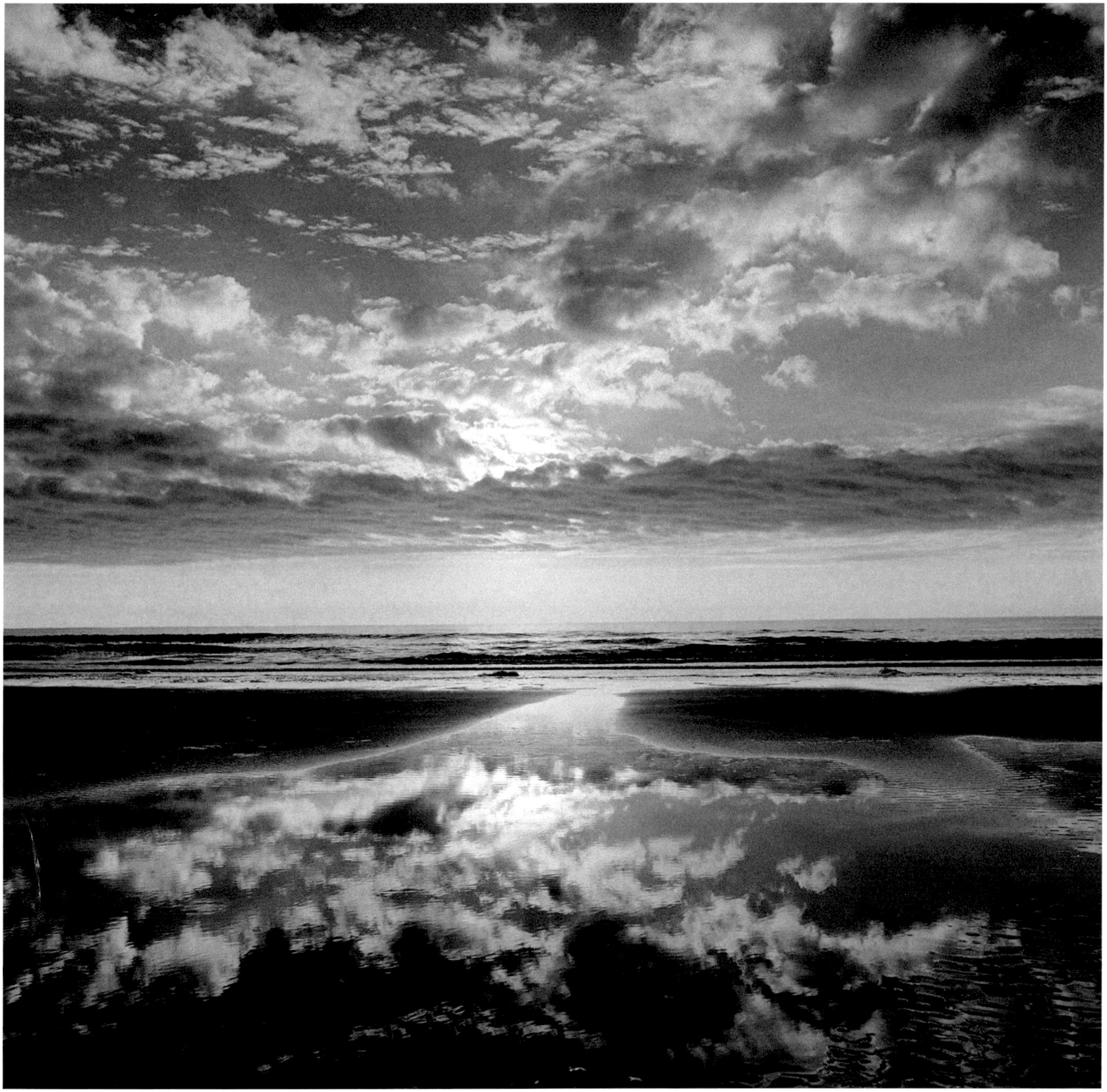

First Light, 2007

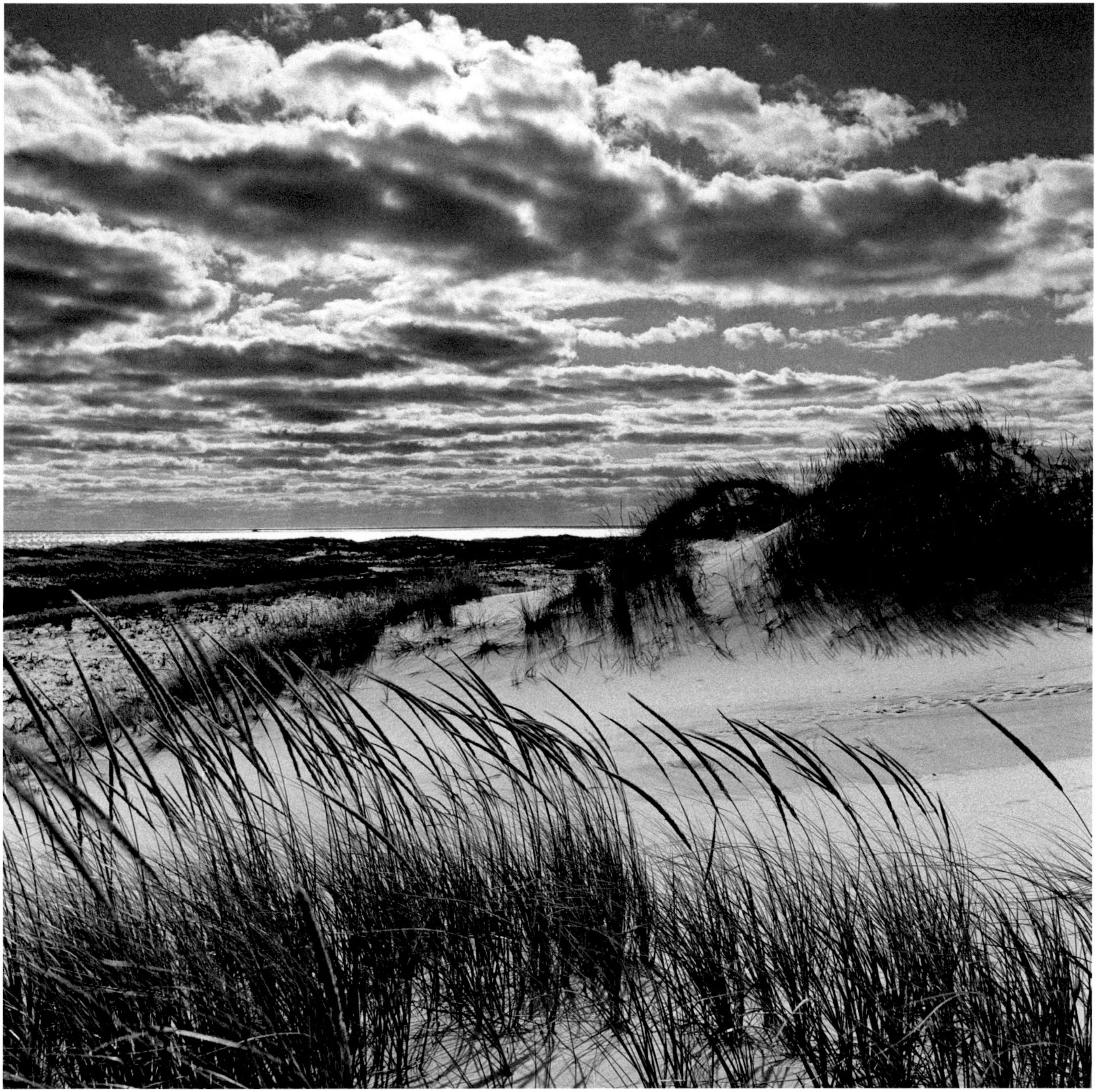

Beyond, 2008

The sea does not reward those who are too anxious, too greedy, or too impatient. . . . One should lie empty, open, choiceless as a beach . . .

—ANNE MORROW LINDBERGH

Island Dunes, 2018

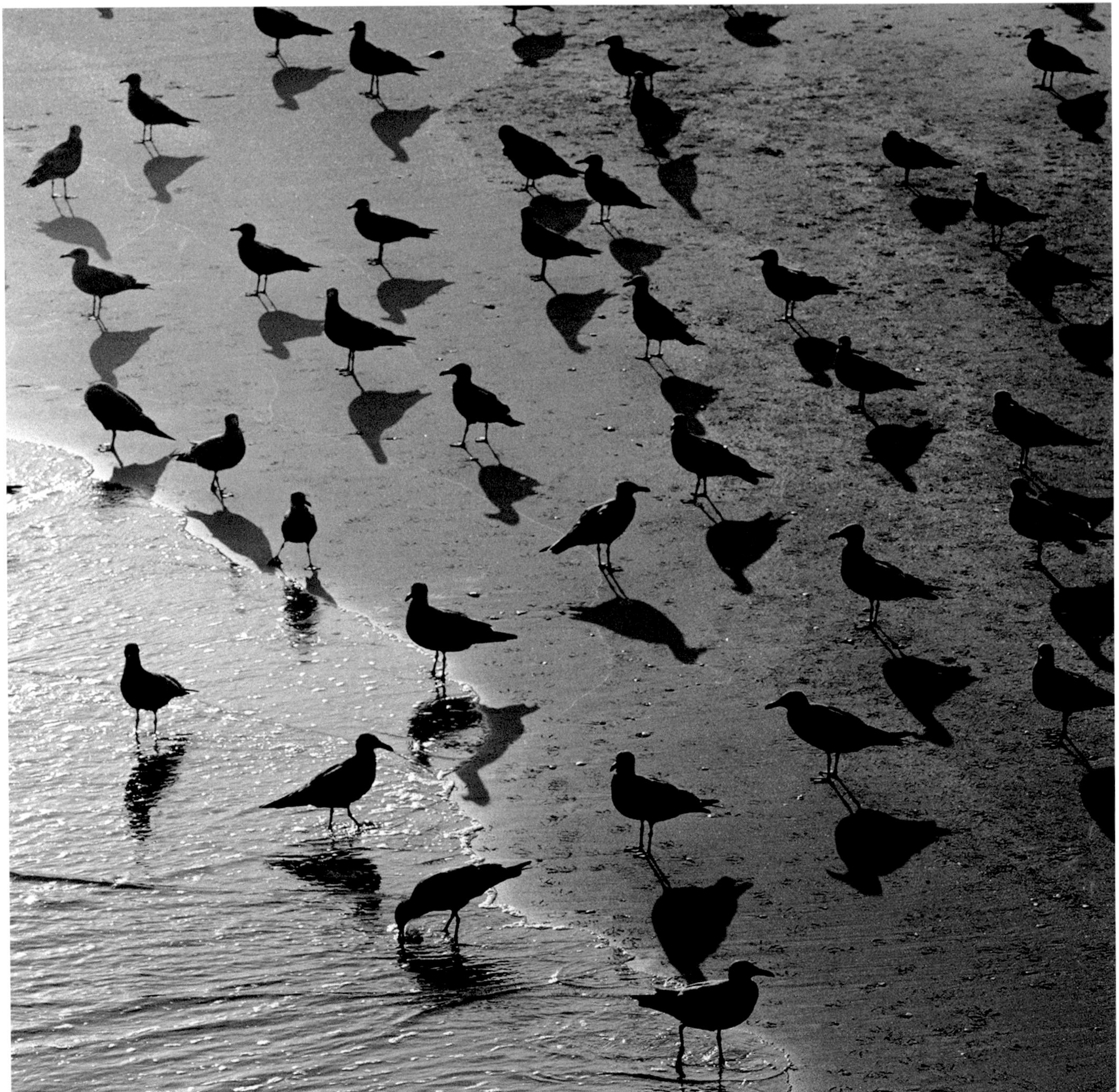

Escher's Seagulls, 2005

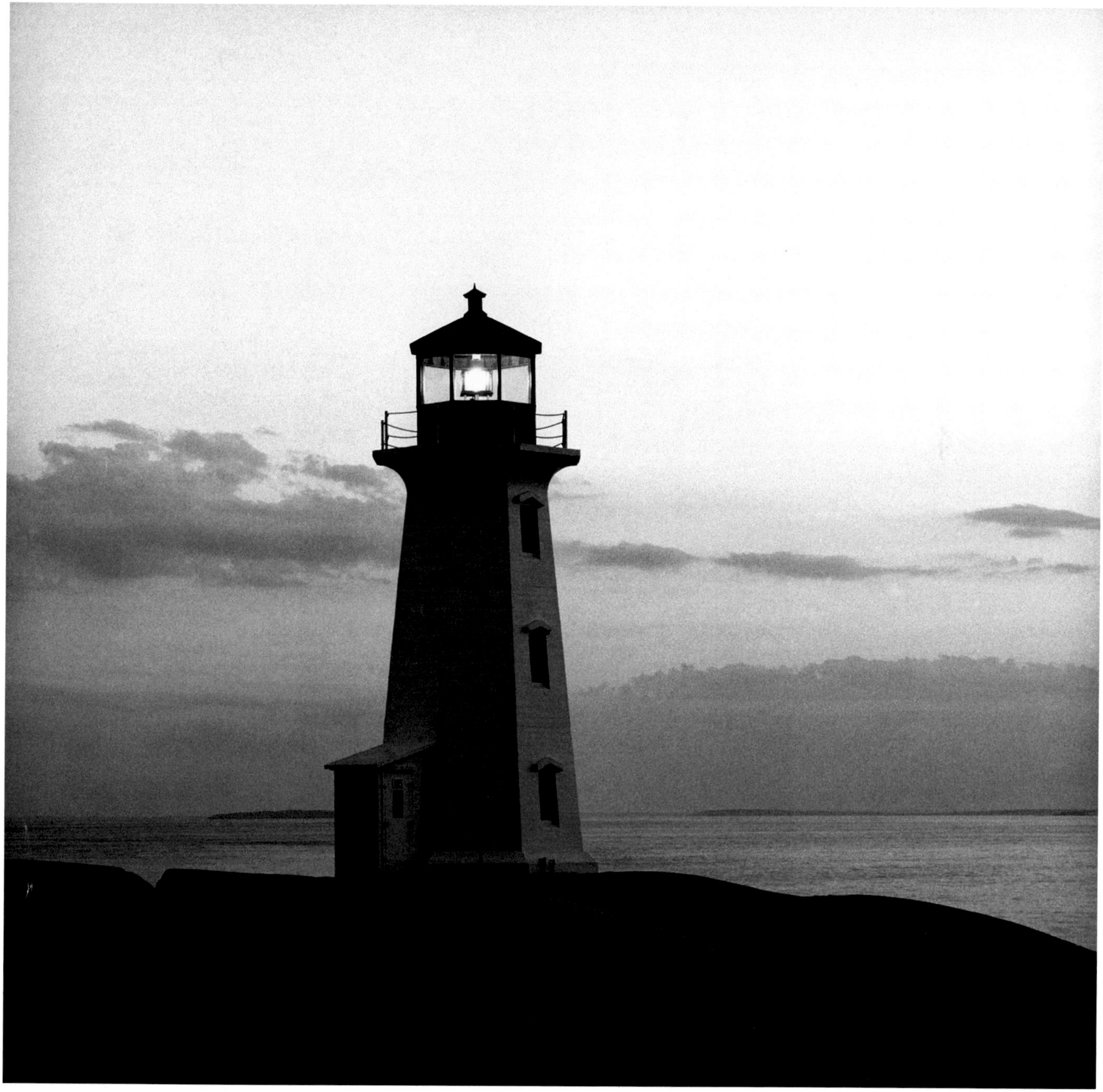

Peggy's Cove Light, 1998

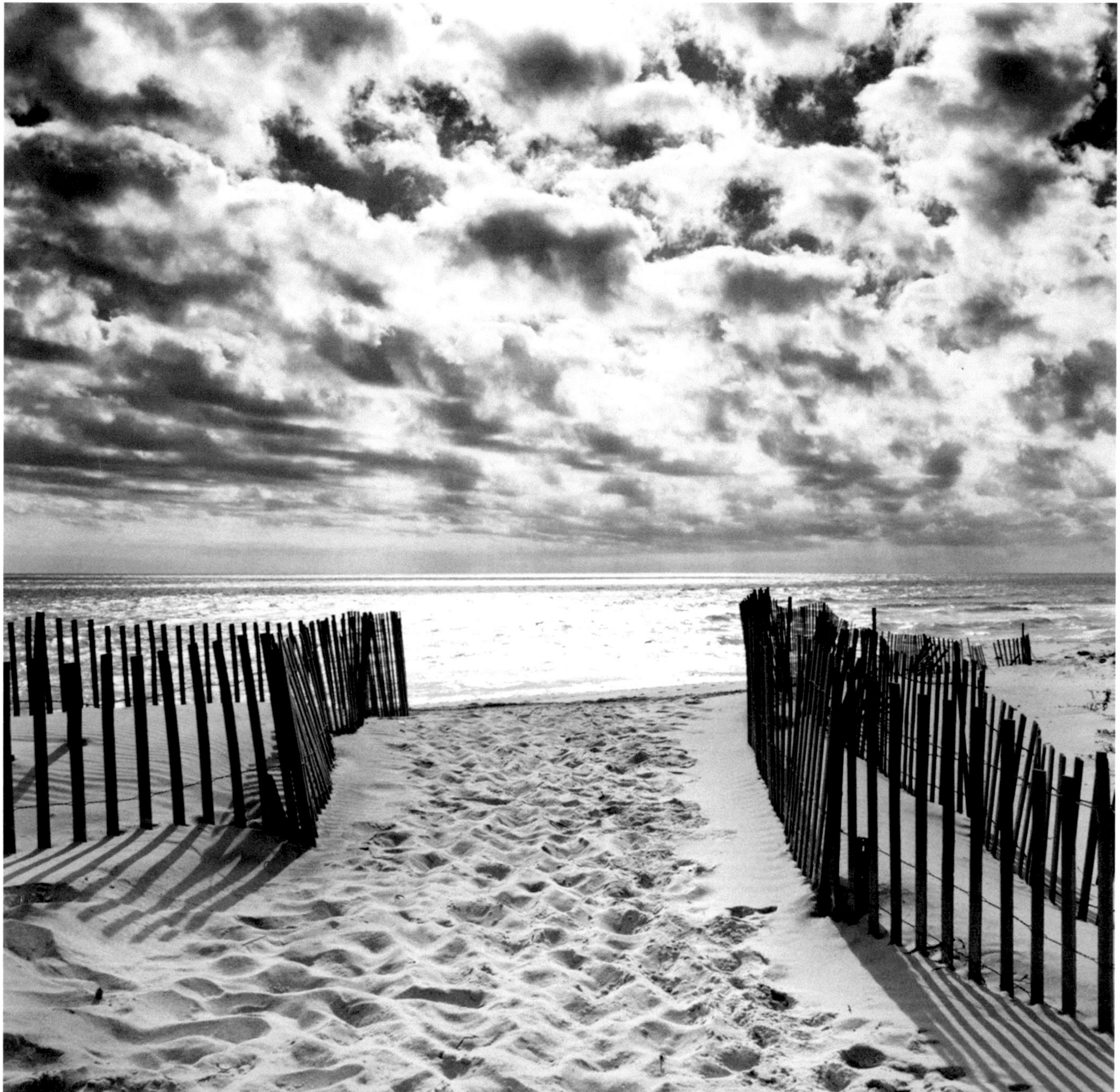

South Beach, 2001

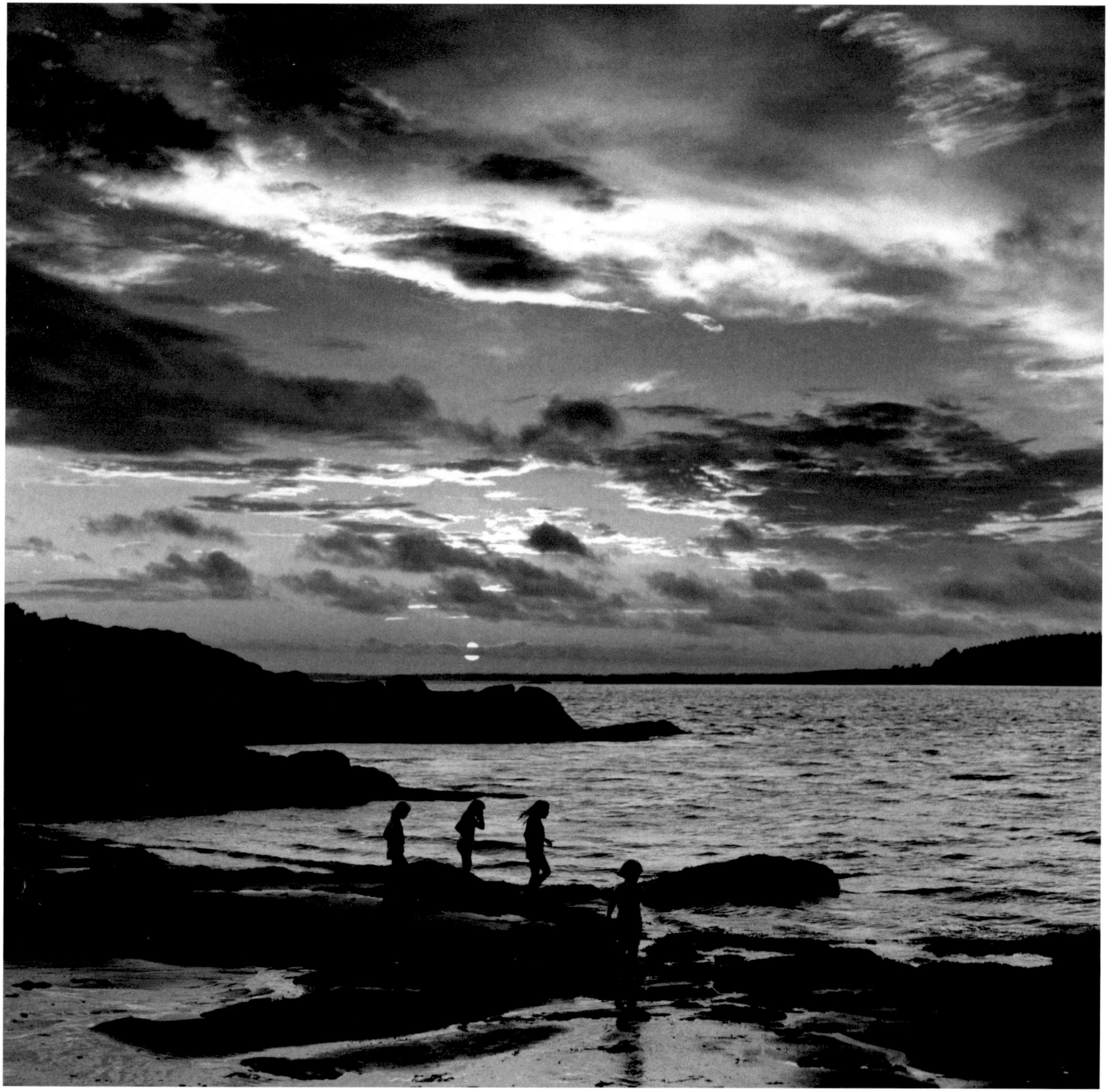

Playing at Sunset, Hermit Island, 2012

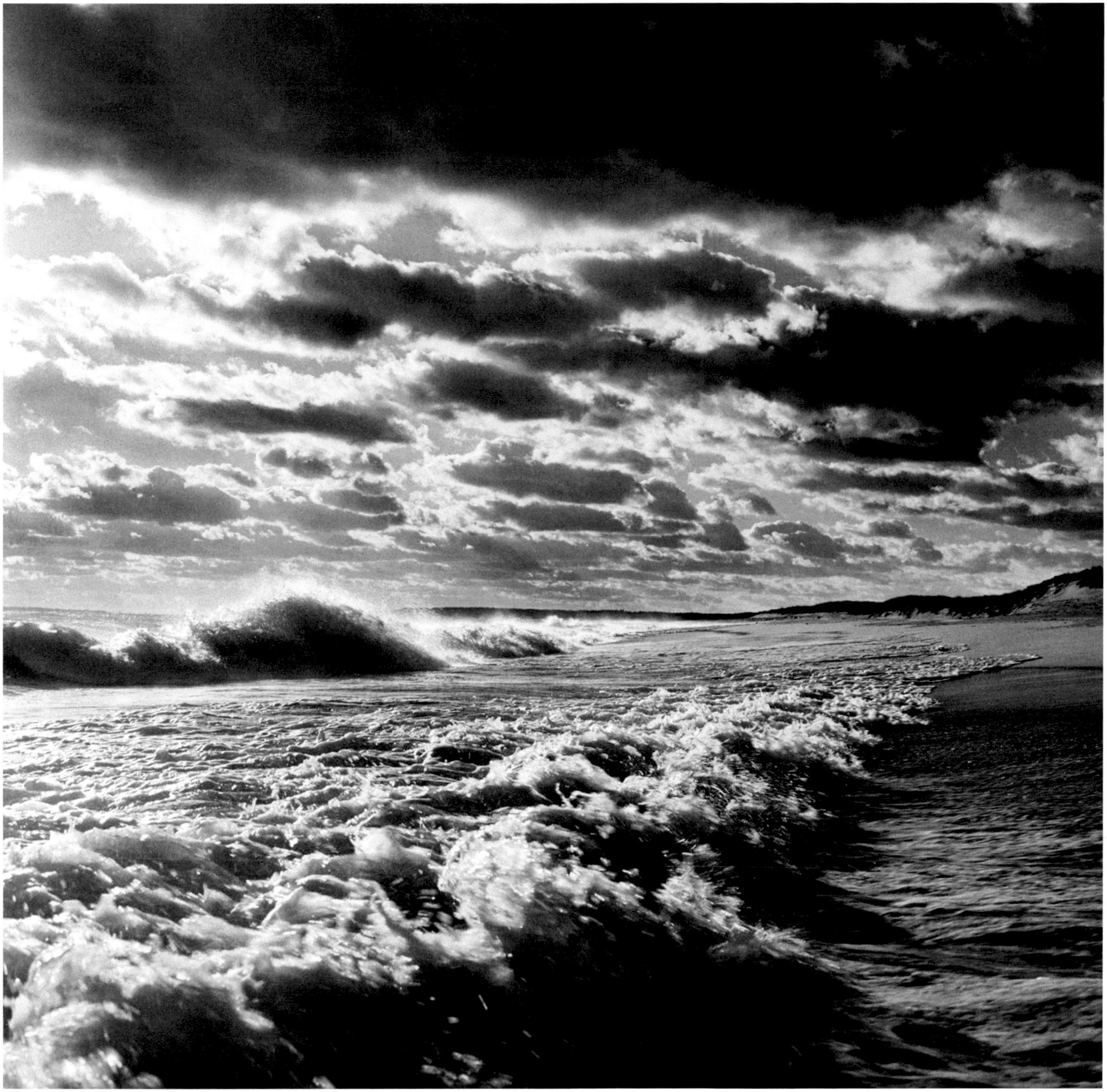

Surf, 2002

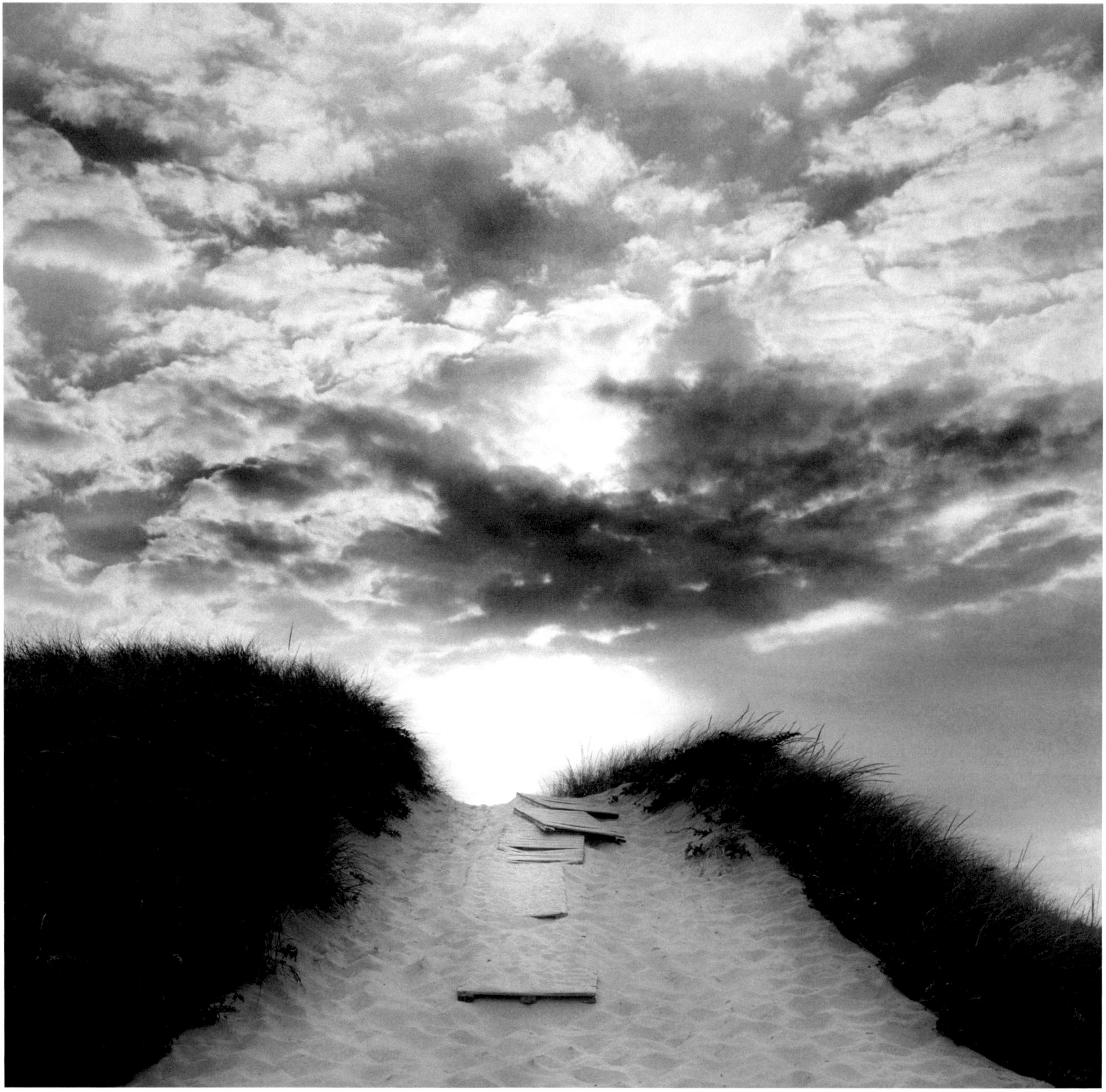

Pathway to the Beach, 1998

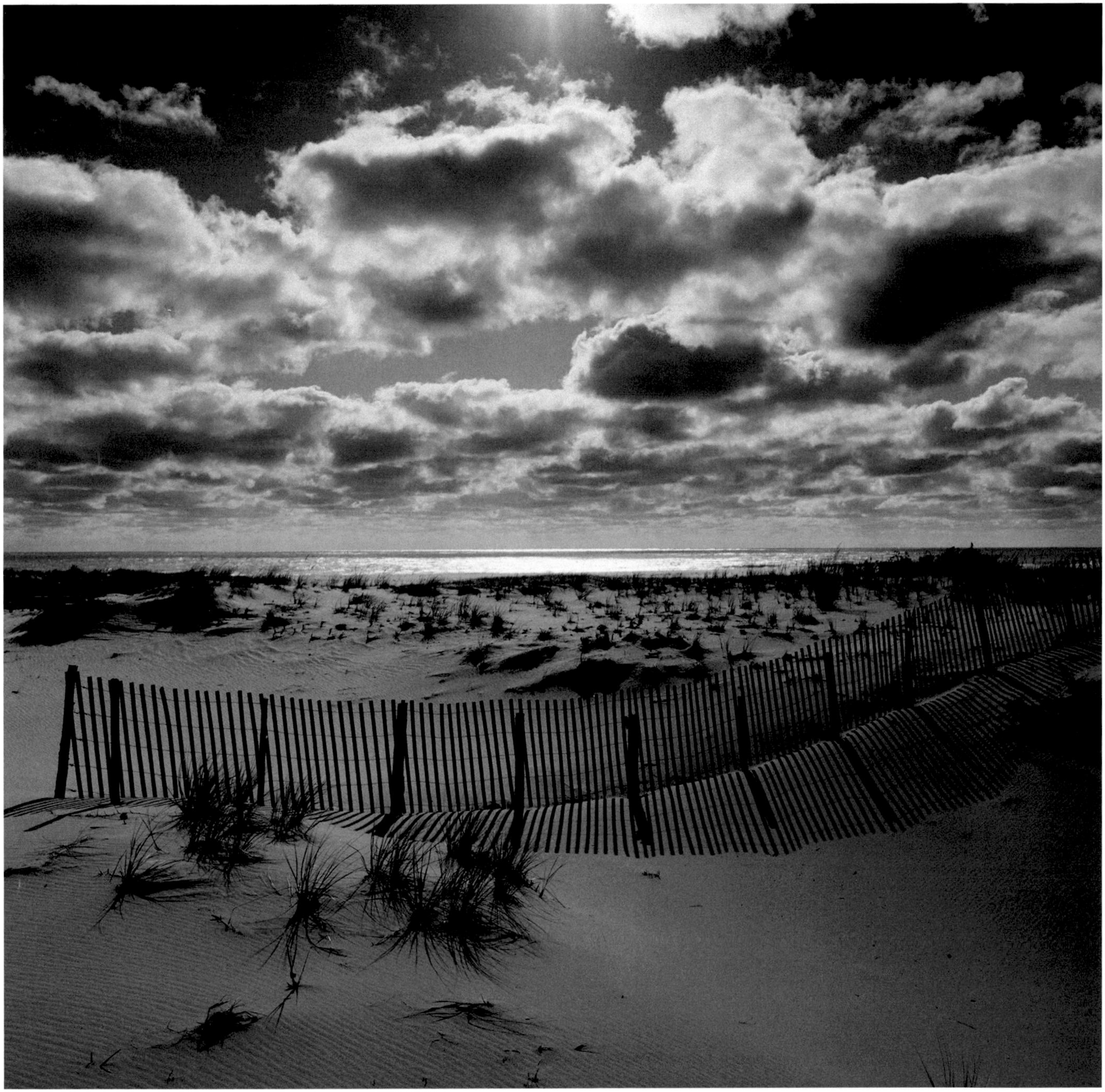

Autumn Visit, 2011

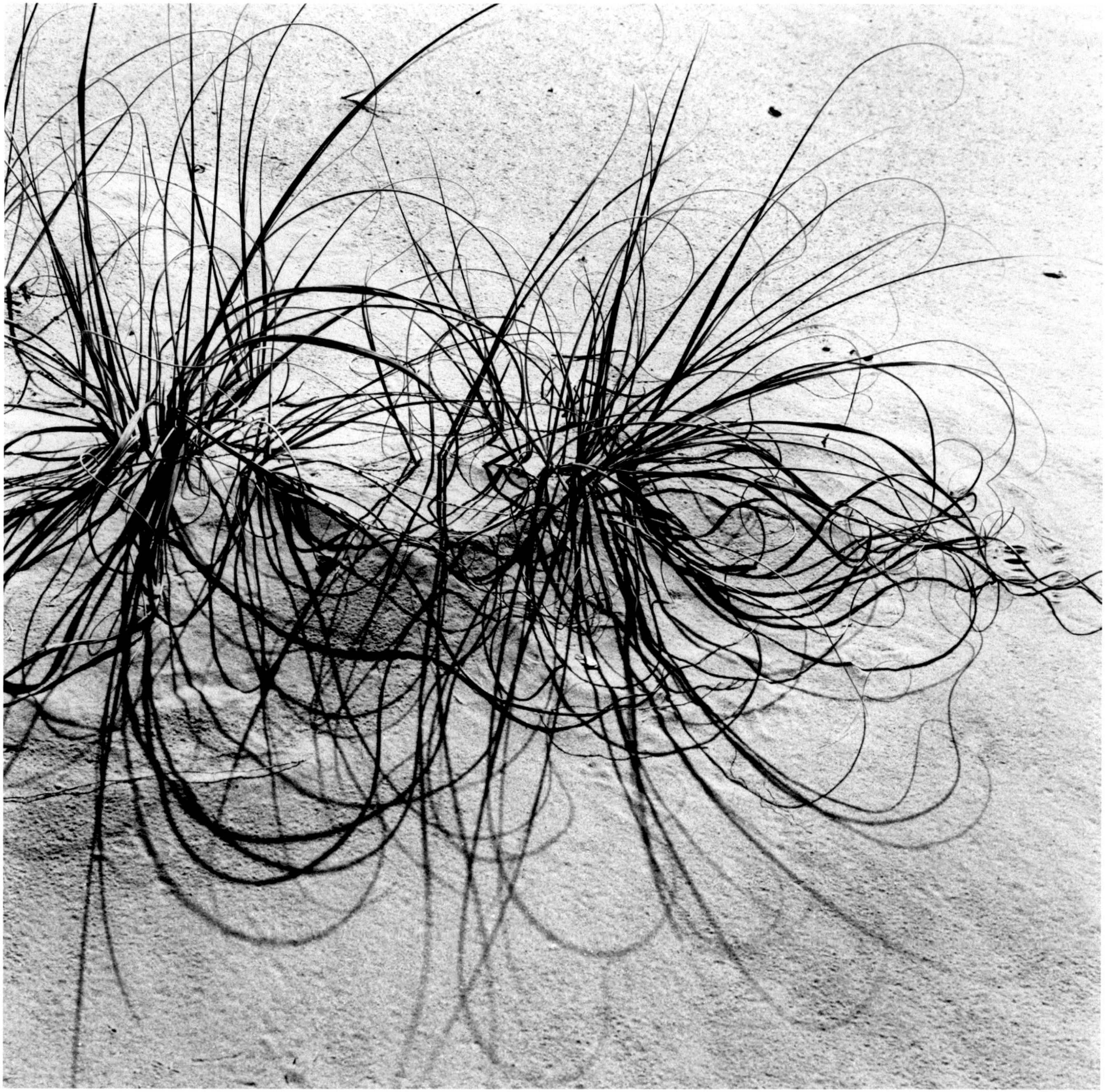

Dune Grass, 2012

A MOMENTARY CREED

I believe in the ordinary day
that is here at this moment and is me

I do not see it going its own way
but I never saw how it came to me

it extends beyond whatever I may
think I know and all that is real to me

it is the present that it bears away
where has it gone when it has gone from me

there is no place I know outside today
except for the unknown all around me

the only presence that appears to stay
everything that I call mine it lent me

even the way that I believe the day
for as long as it is here and is me

—W. S. MERWIN

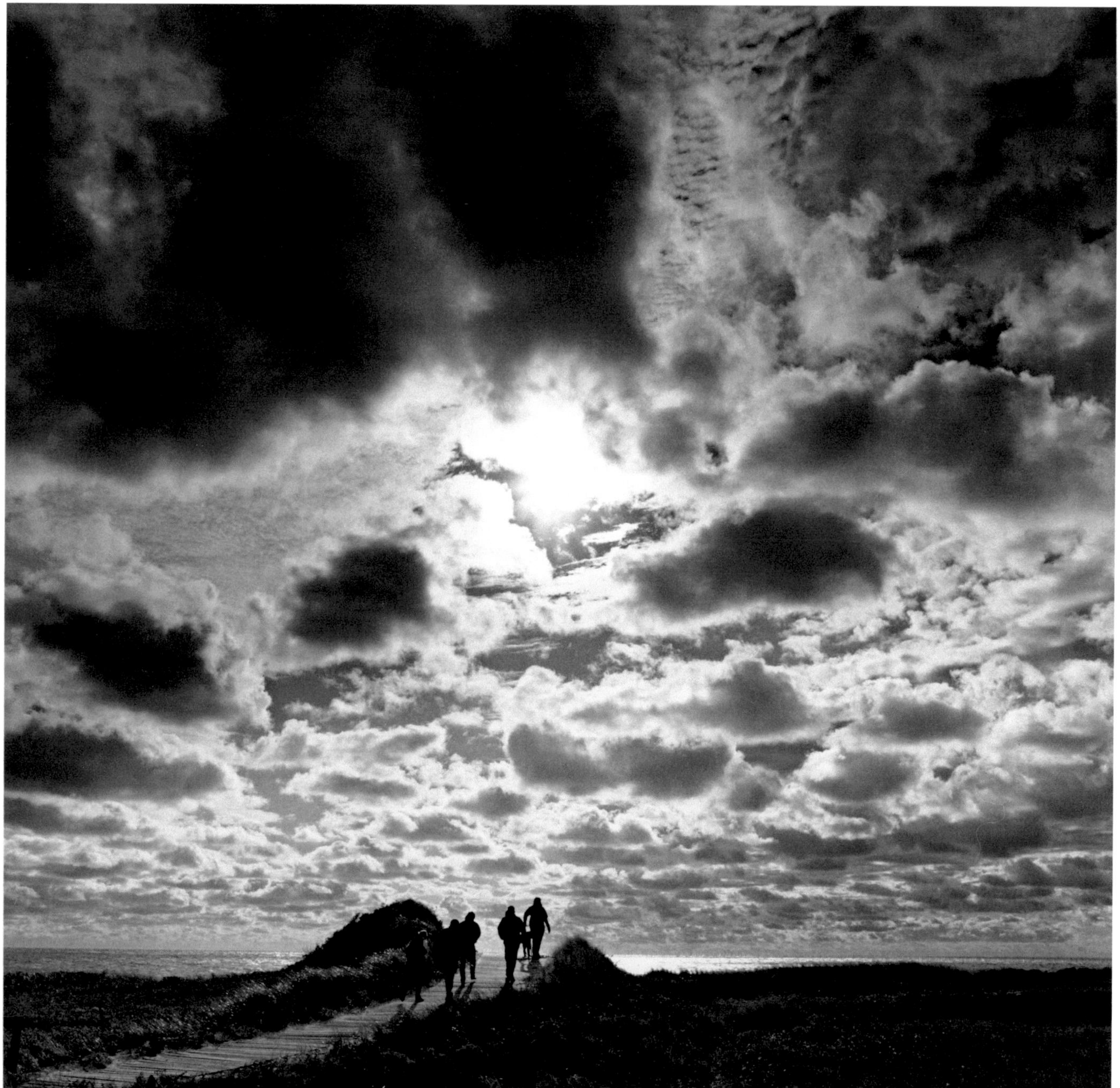

Family Visit, 2012

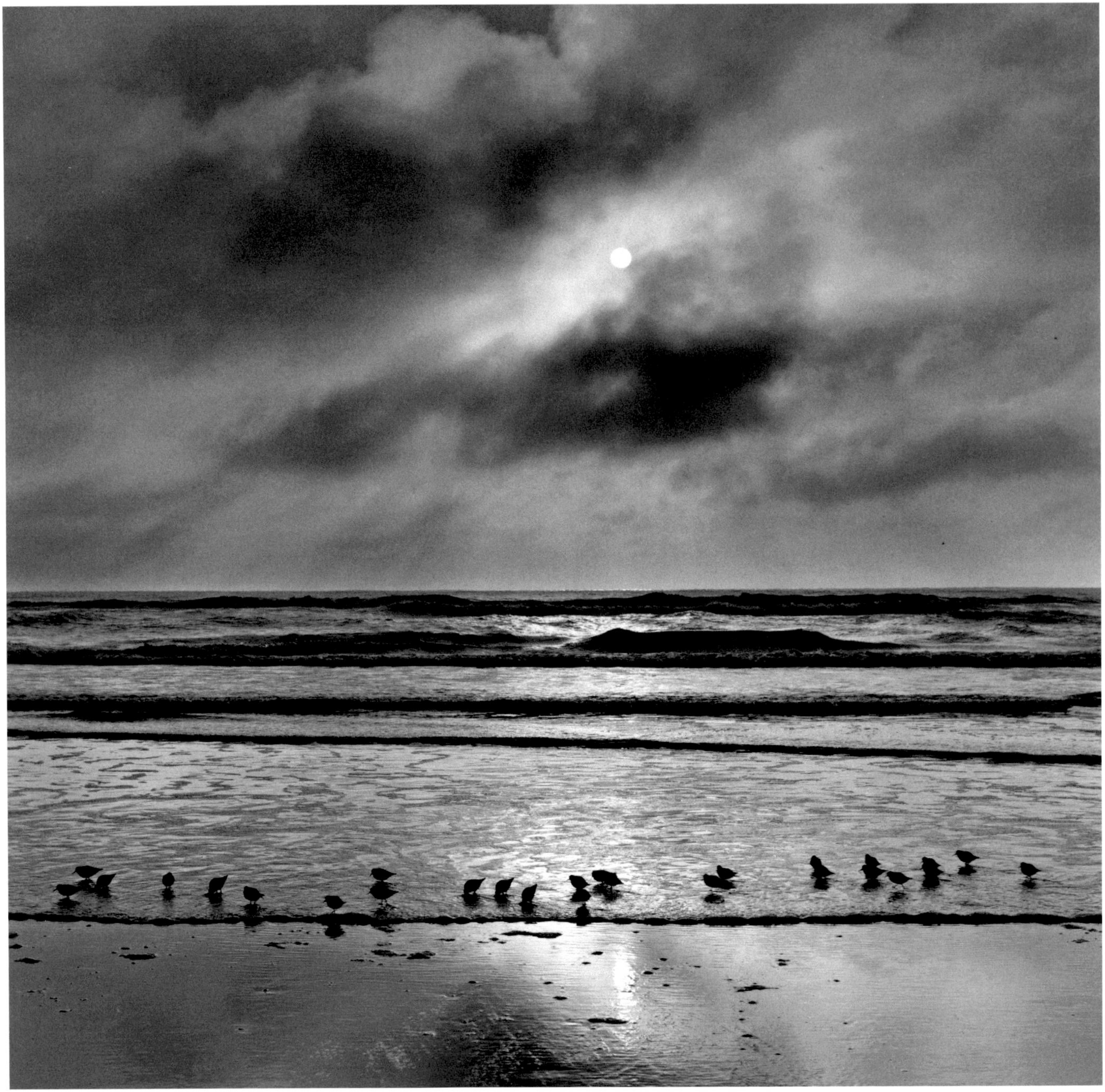

Shore Birds, 2015

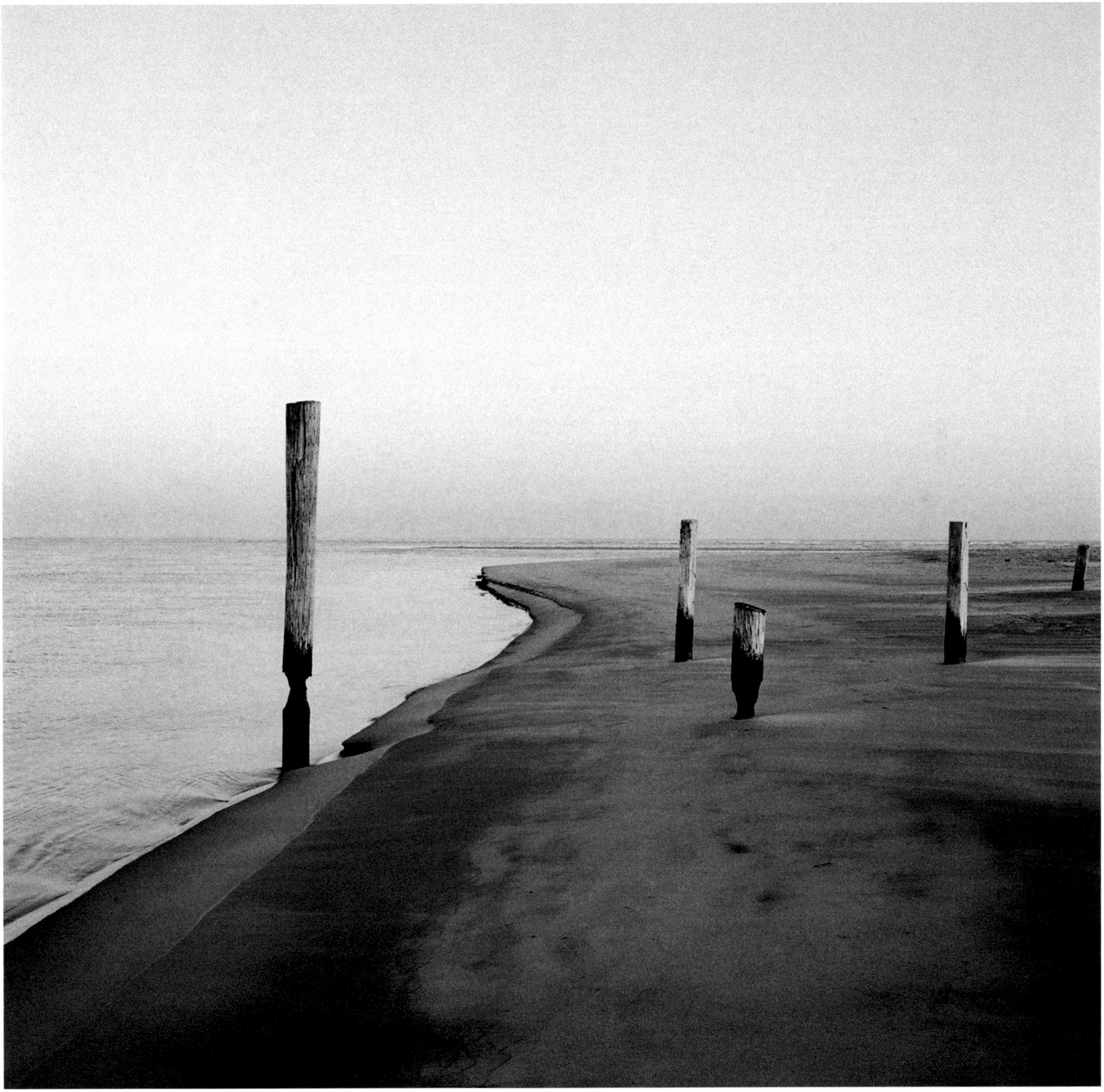

Pilings, 2007

Evening Waves, 2007

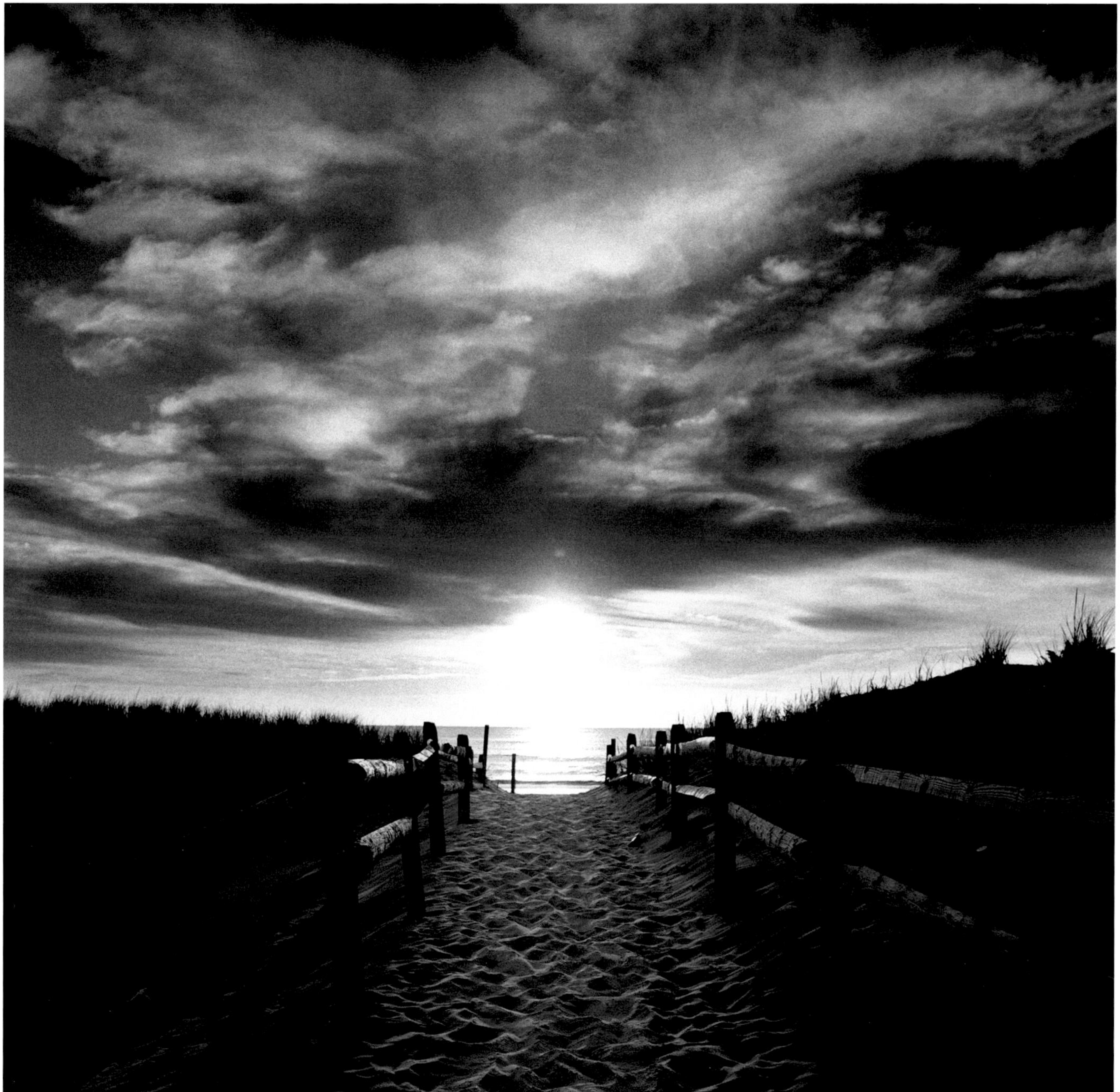

Serenity, Island Beach State Park, 2008

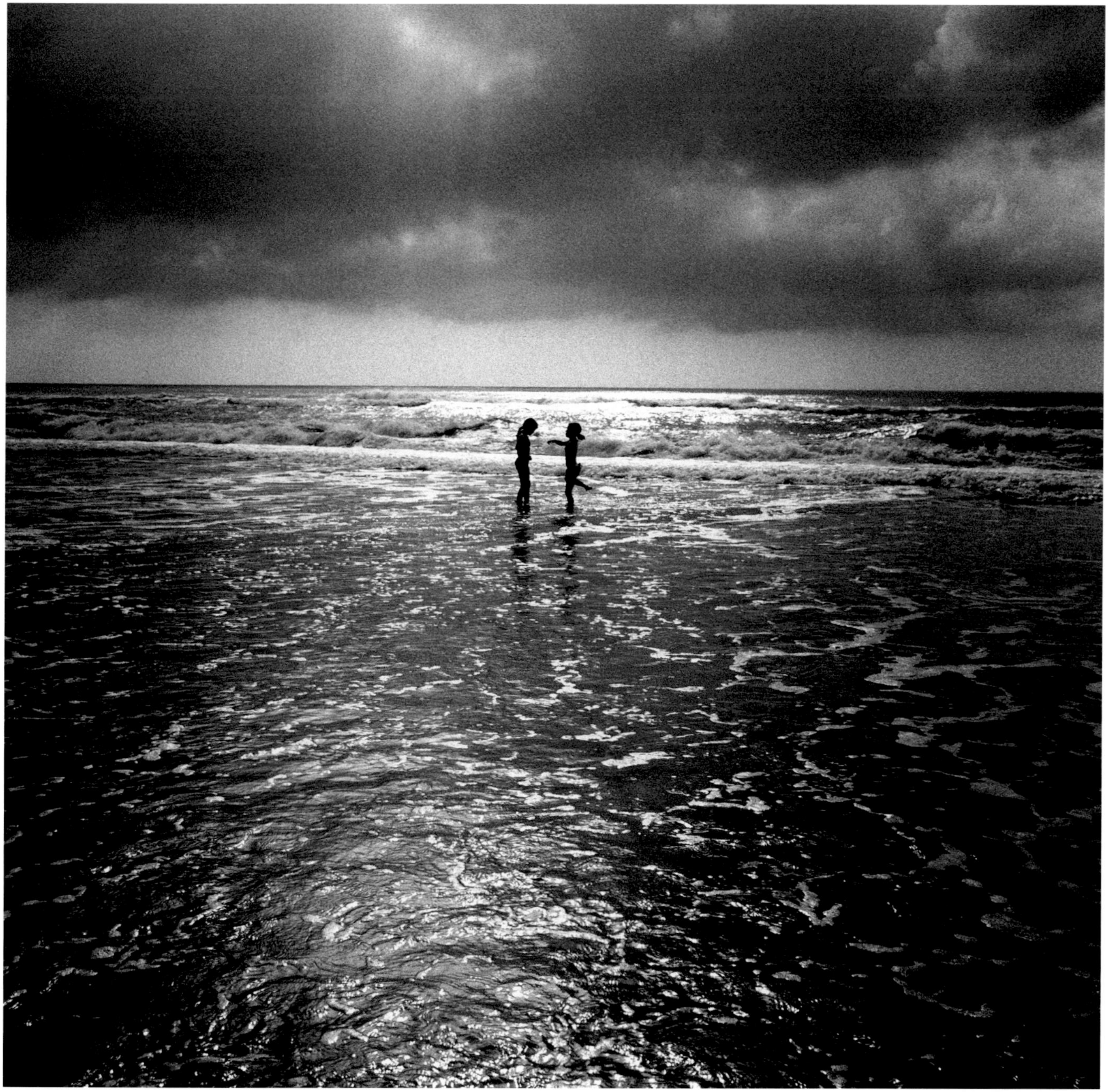

Friends, 2008

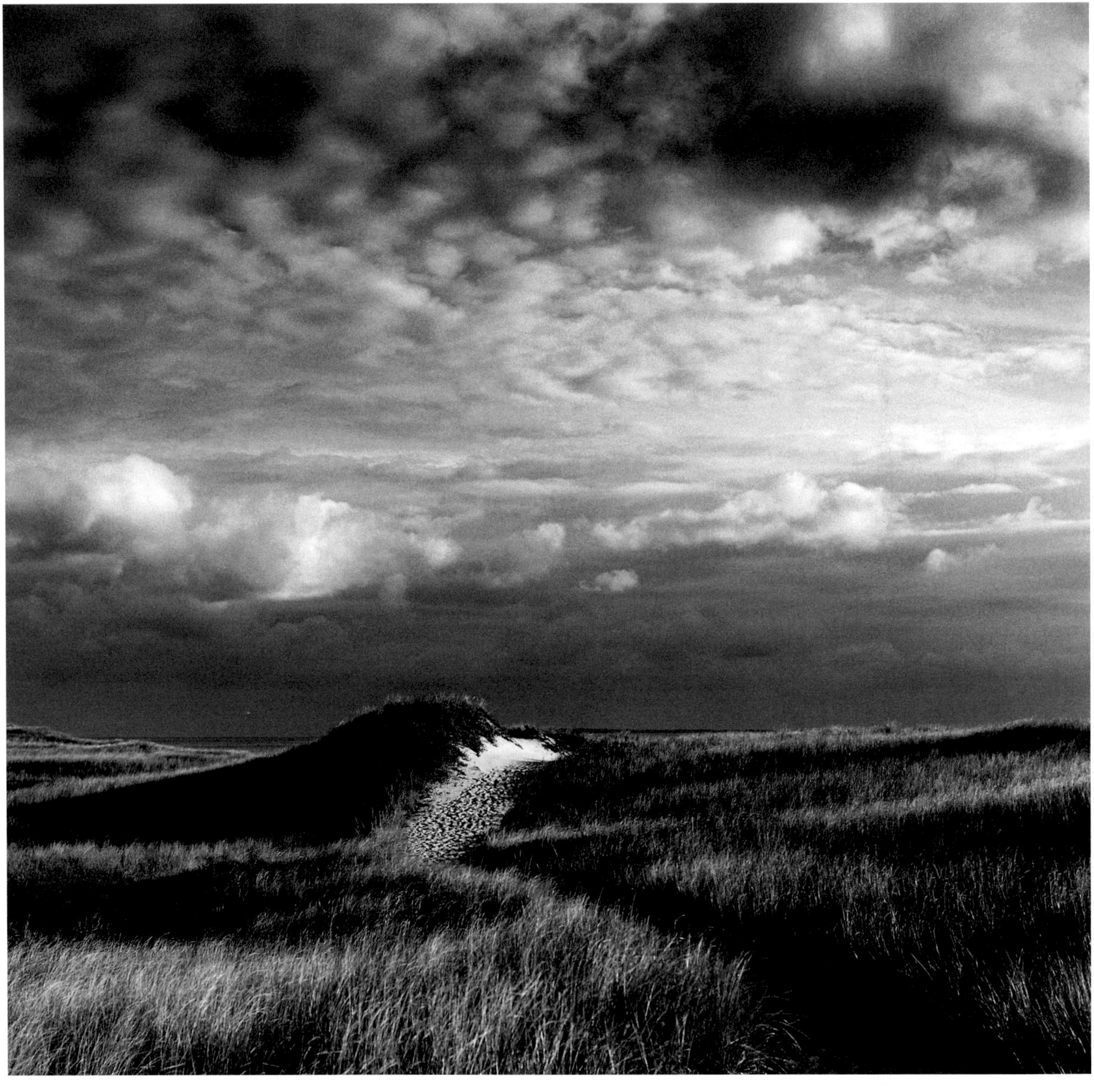

Dune Path, 2004

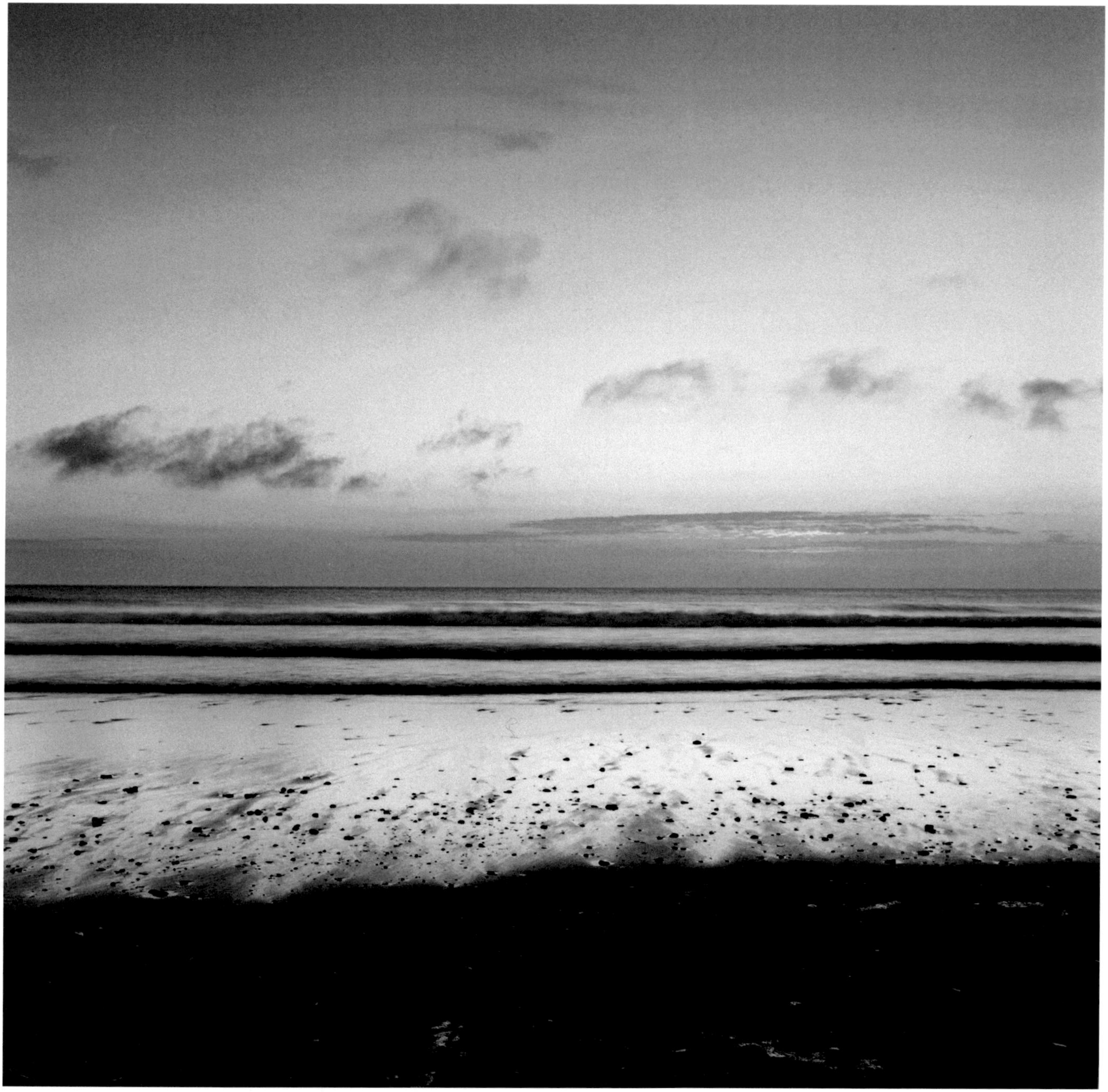

Three Waves, 2014

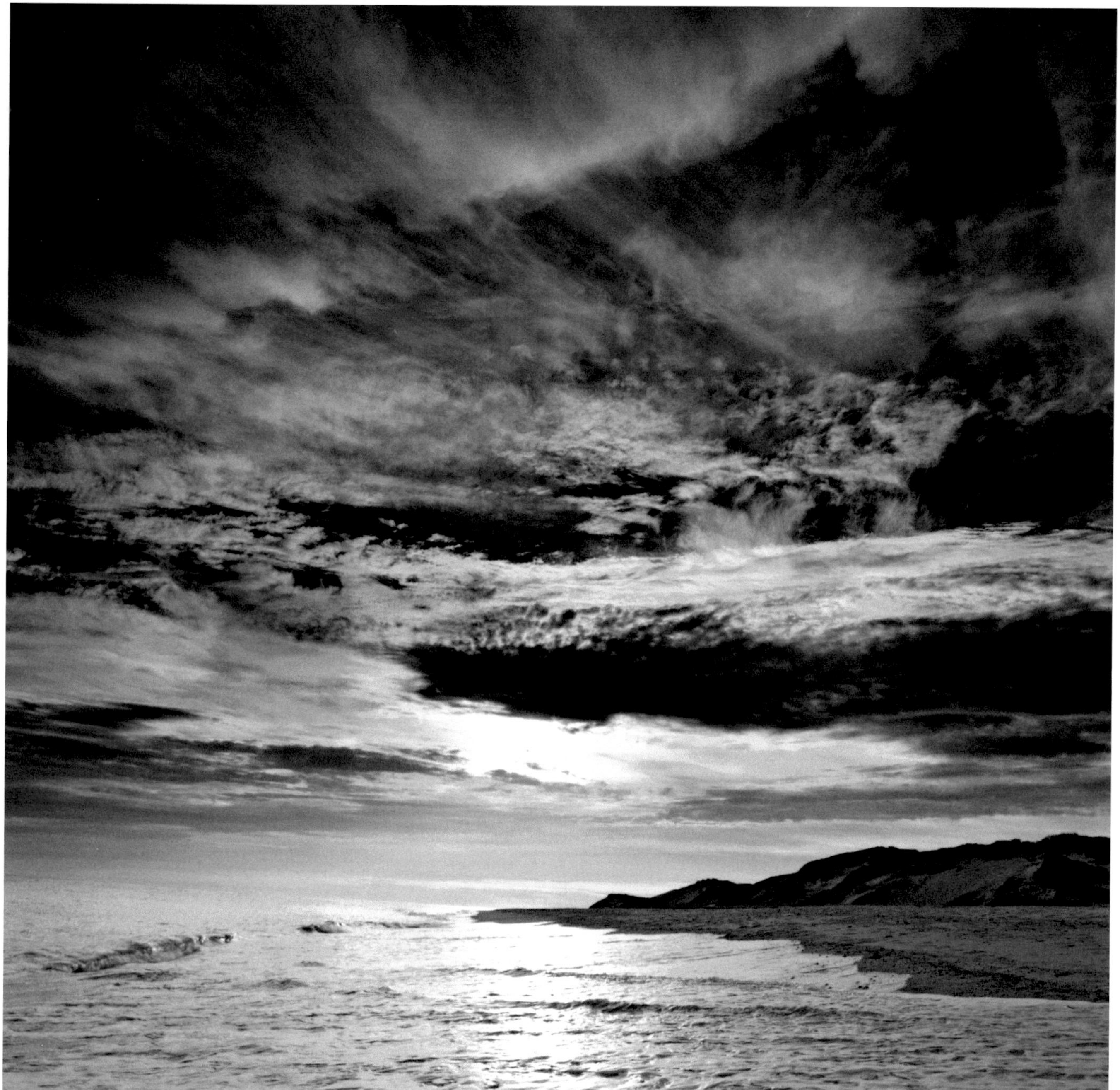

Atlantic Dunes, 2015

The sea, once it casts its spell, holds one in its net of wonder forever.

—JACQUES-YVES COUSTEAU

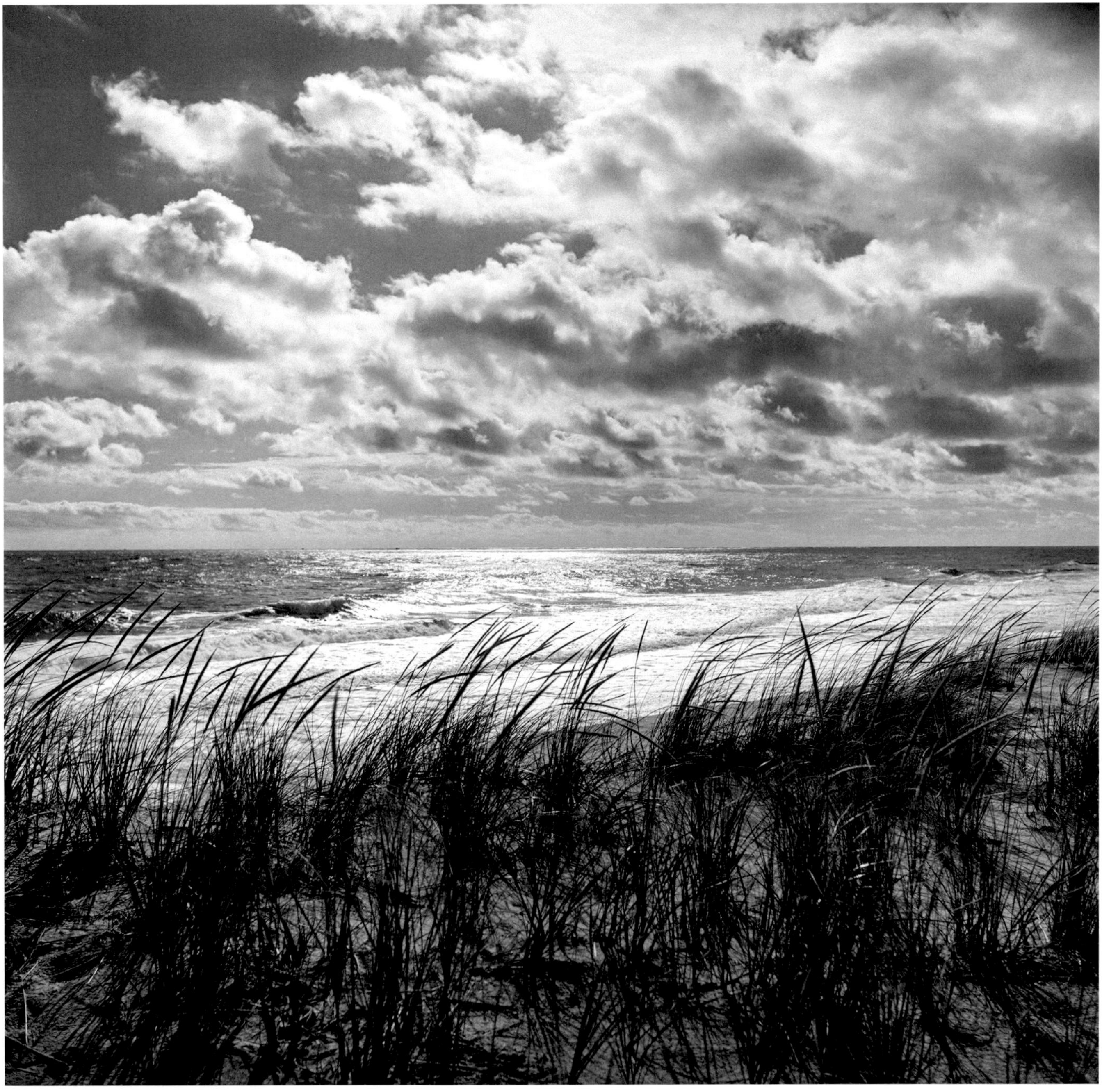

Dune Grass, 2017

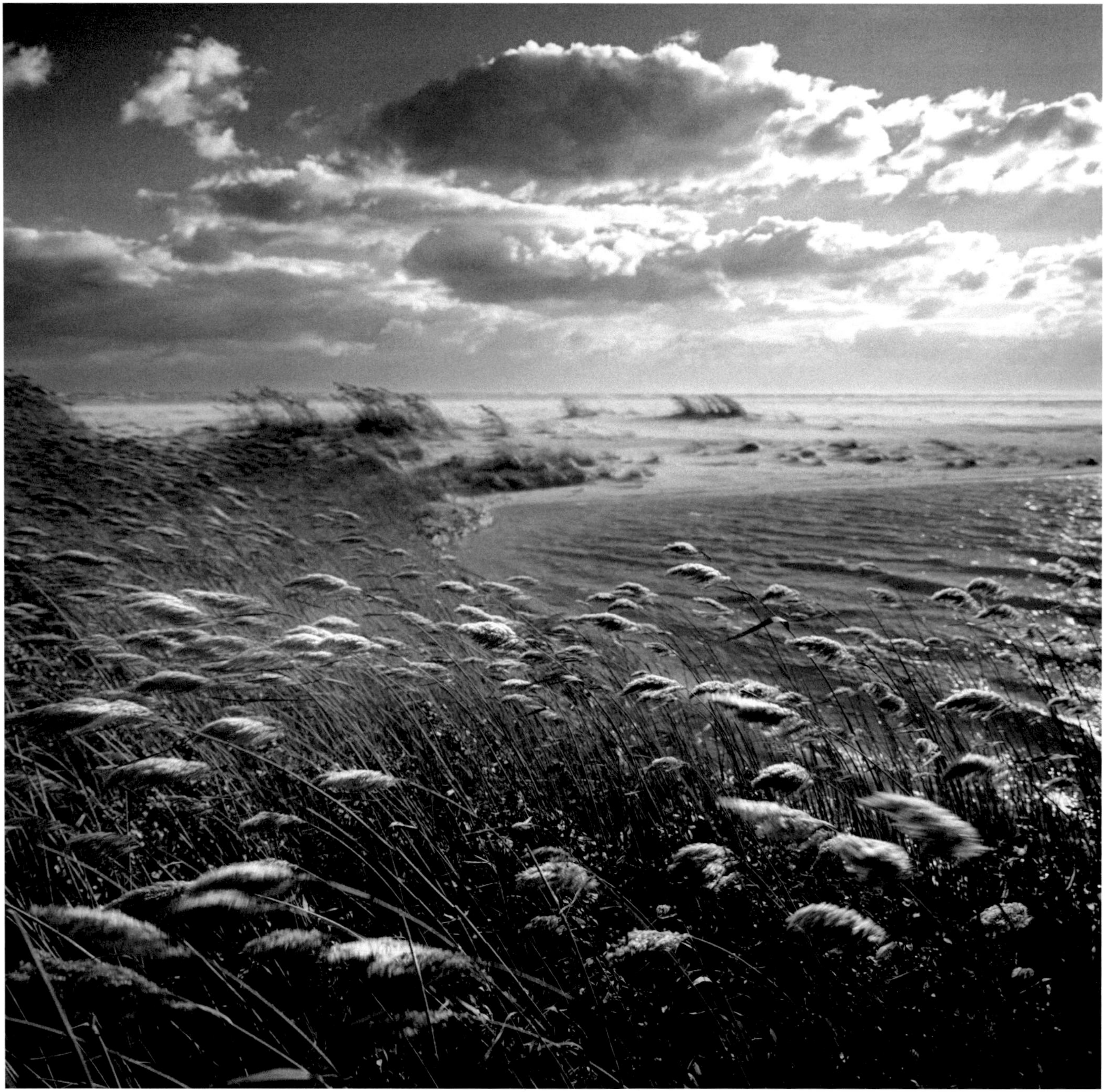

Phragmites, 2003

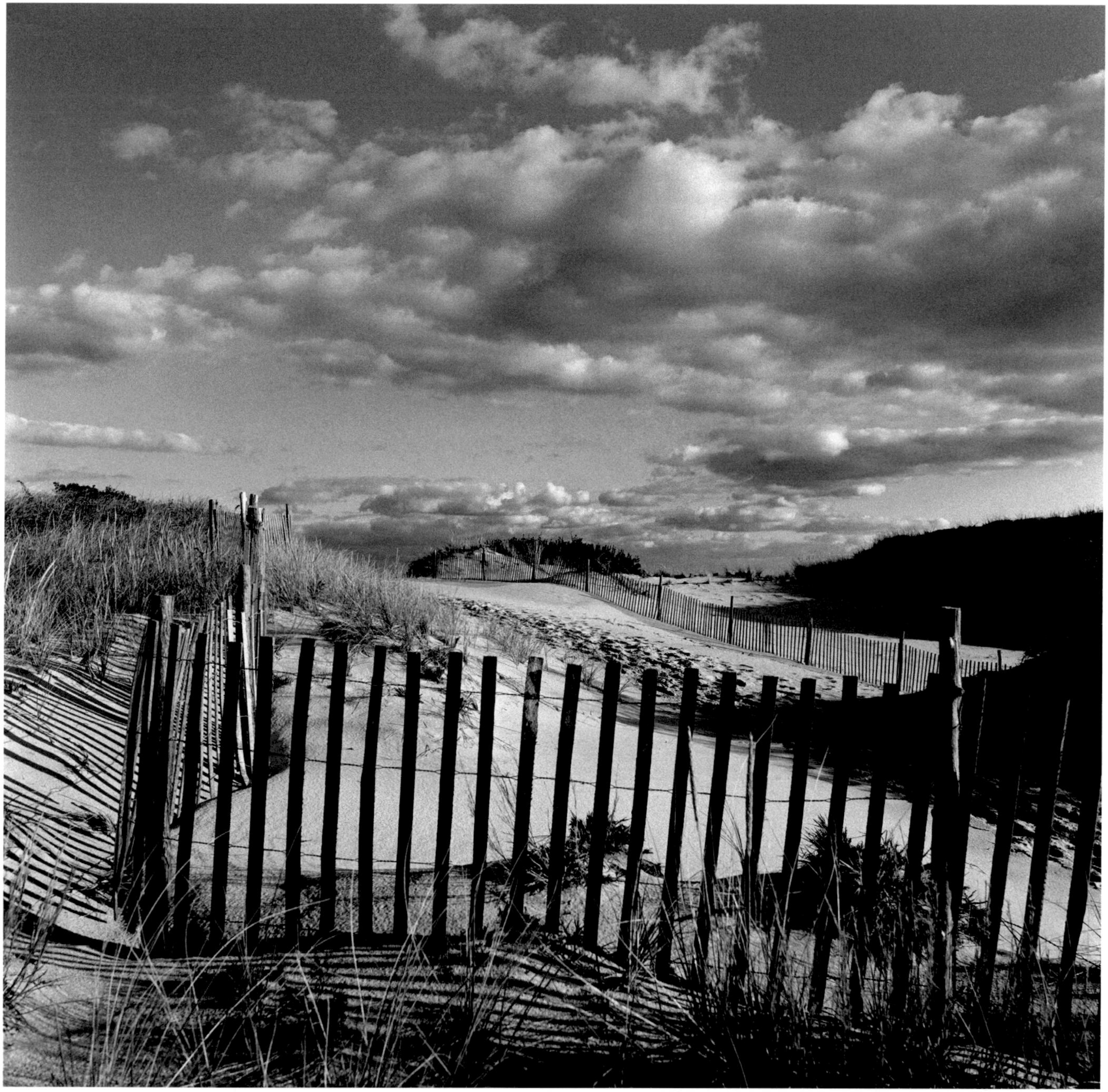

Shifting Sand, 2007

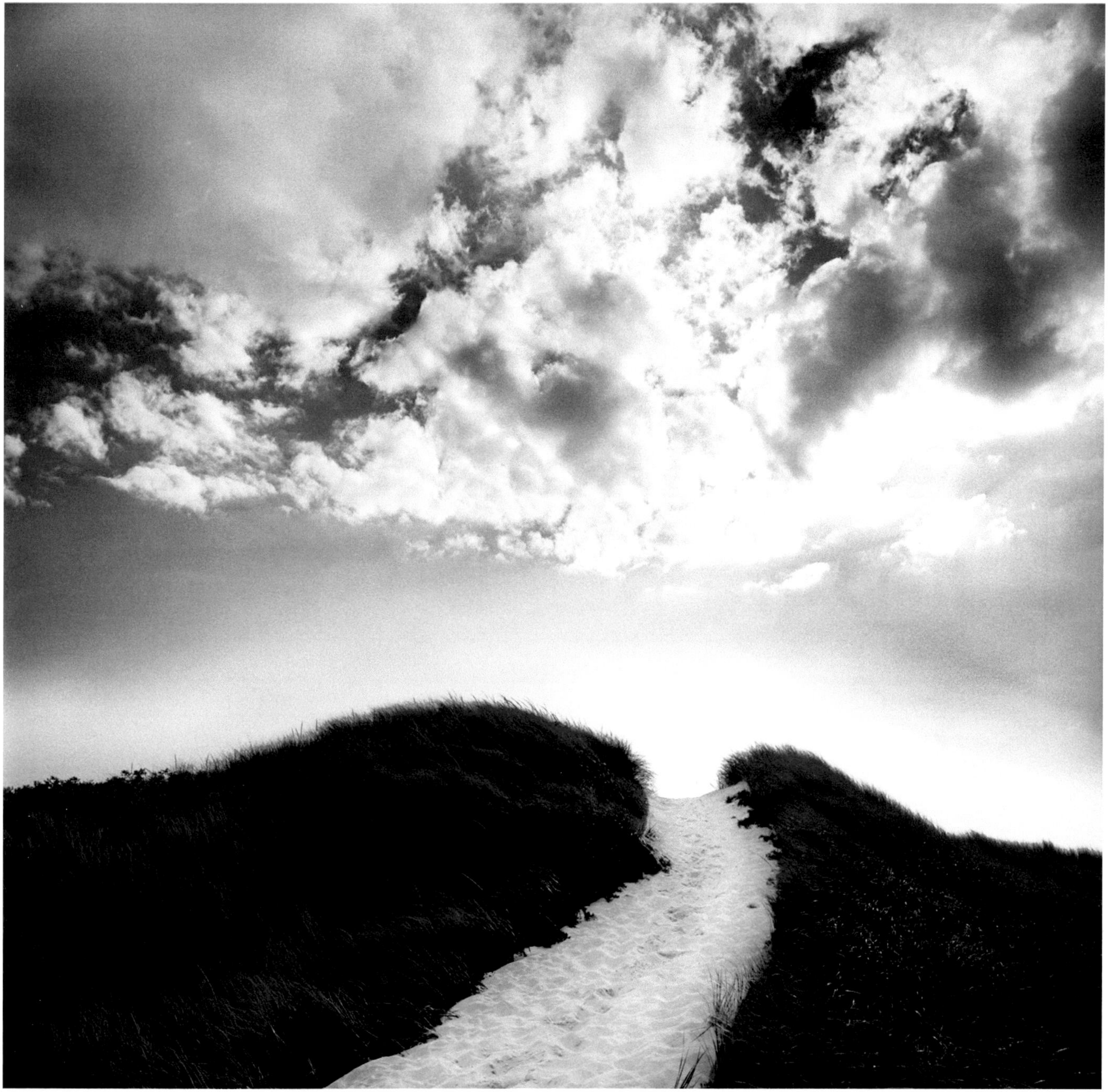

Winter Dune, 2000

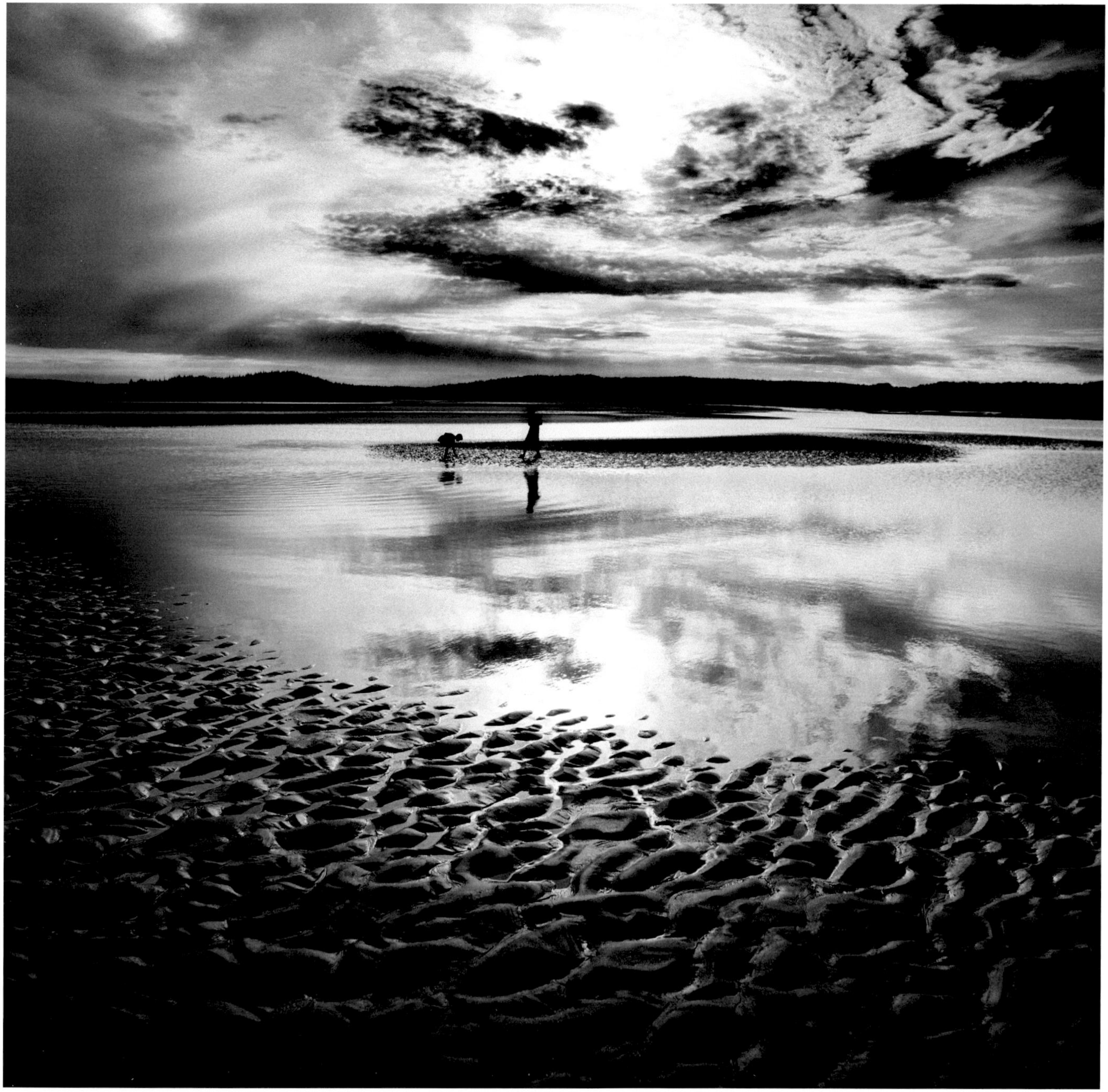

Treasure Hunt, 2002

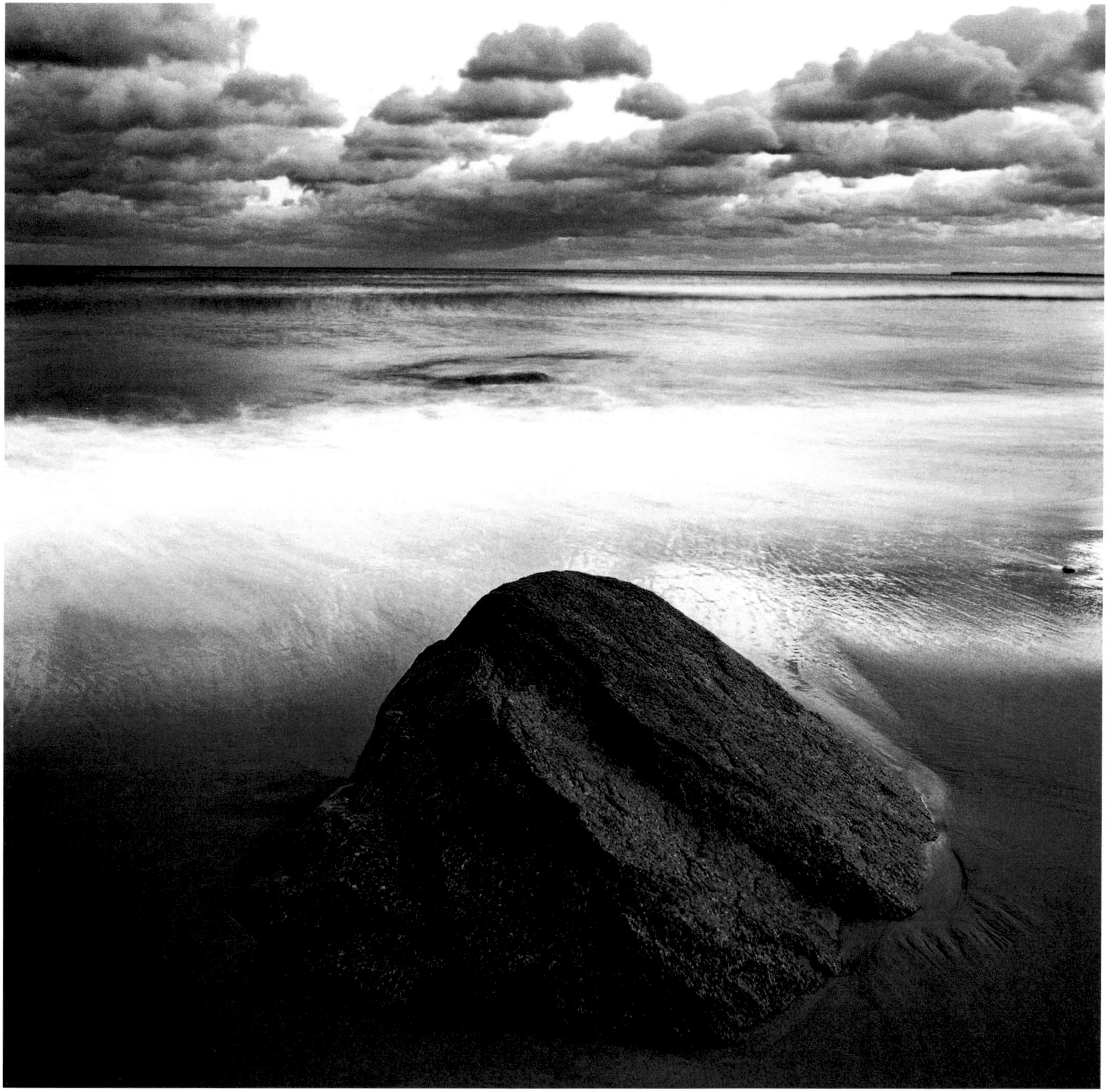

Nomans Land, 1999

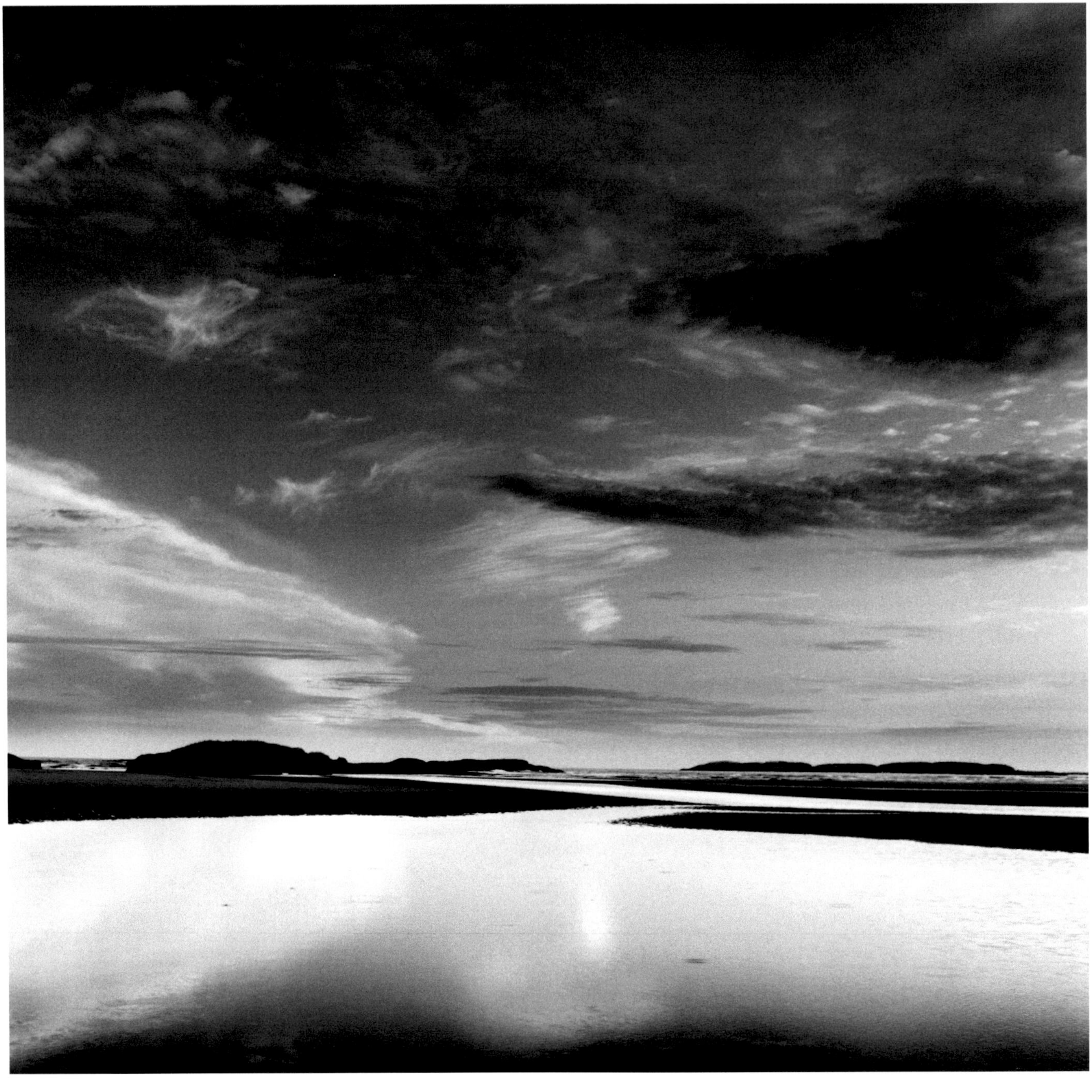

Mirror, 2002

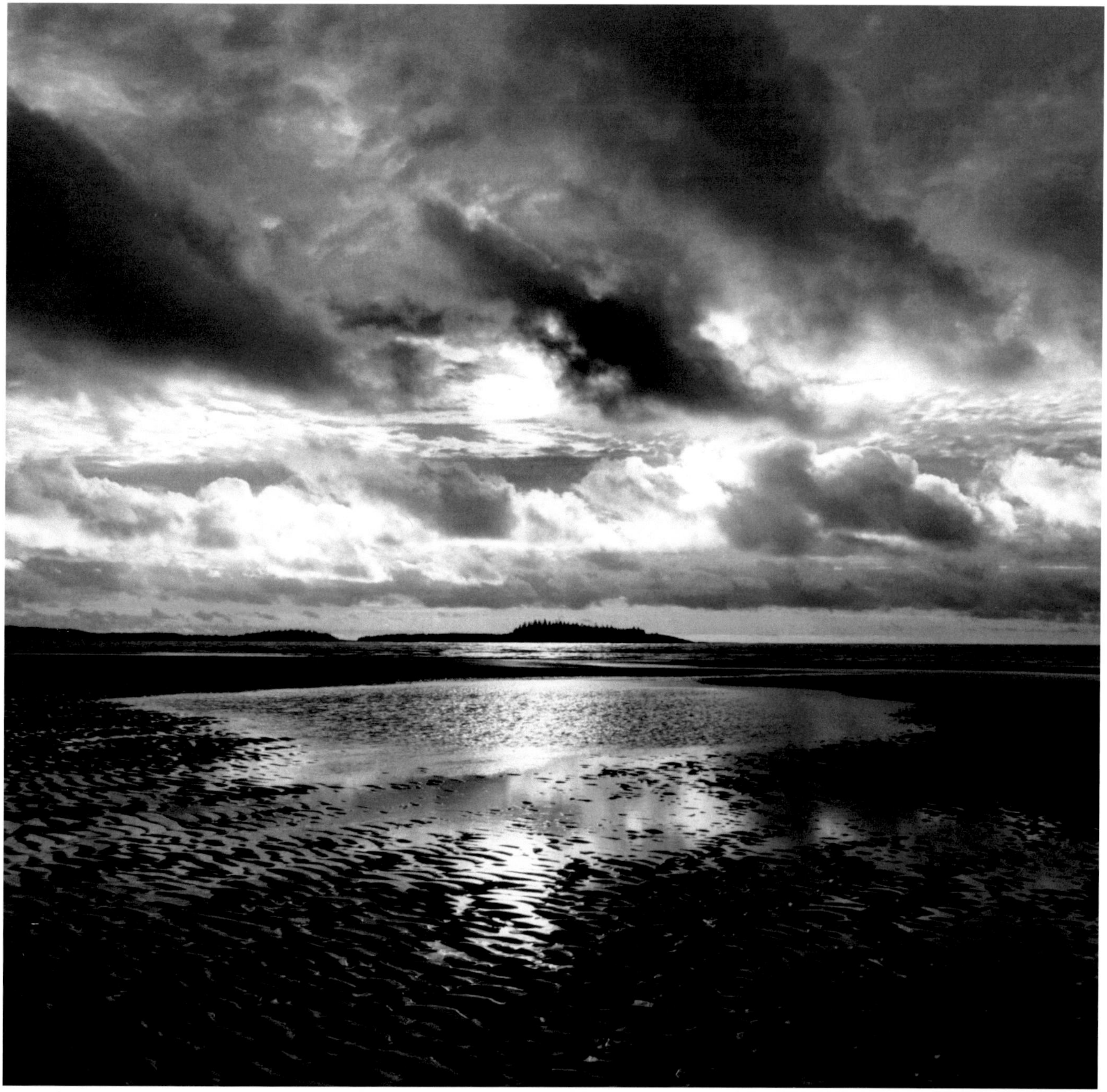

Outgoing Tide, 2018

NEITHER OUT FAR NOR IN DEEP

The people along the sand
All turn and look one way.
They turn their back on the land.
They look at the sea all day.

As long as it takes to pass
A ship keeps raising its hull;
The wetter ground like glass
Reflects a standing gull.

The land may vary more;
But wherever the truth may be—
The water comes ashore,
And the people look at the sea.

They cannot look out far.
They cannot look in deep.
But when was that ever a bar
To any watch they keep?

—ROBERT FROST

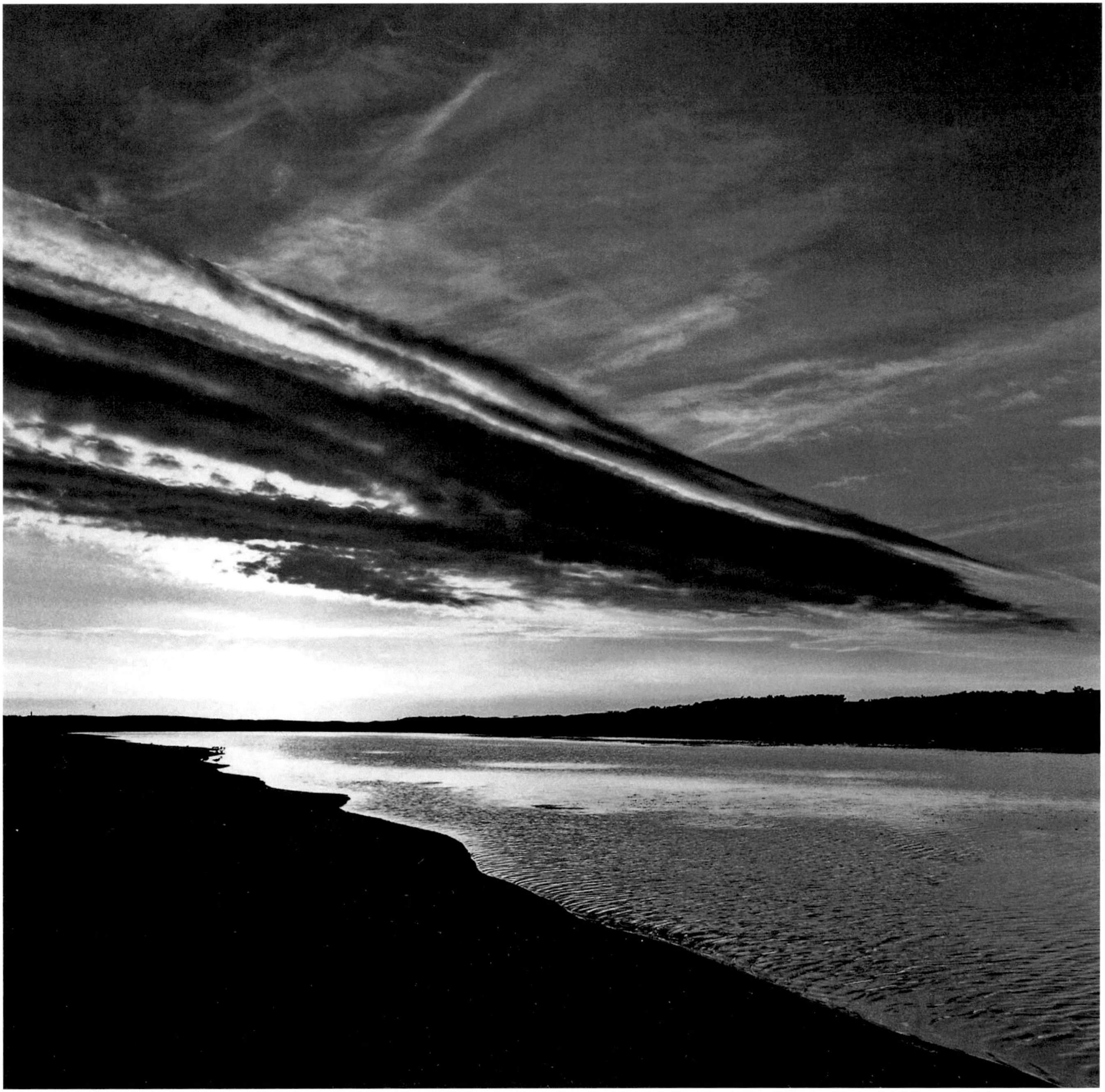

Swan Pond, 1998

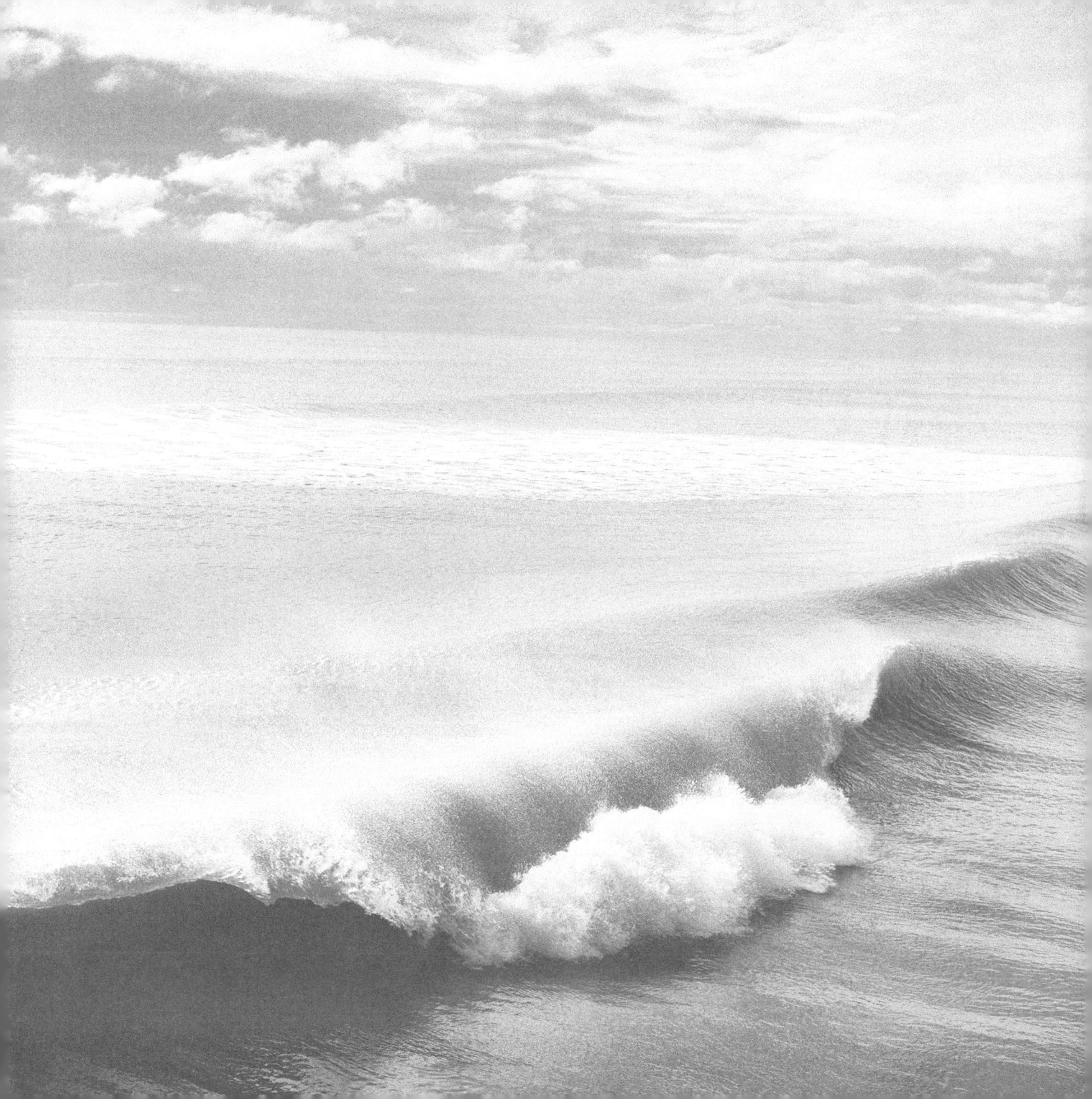

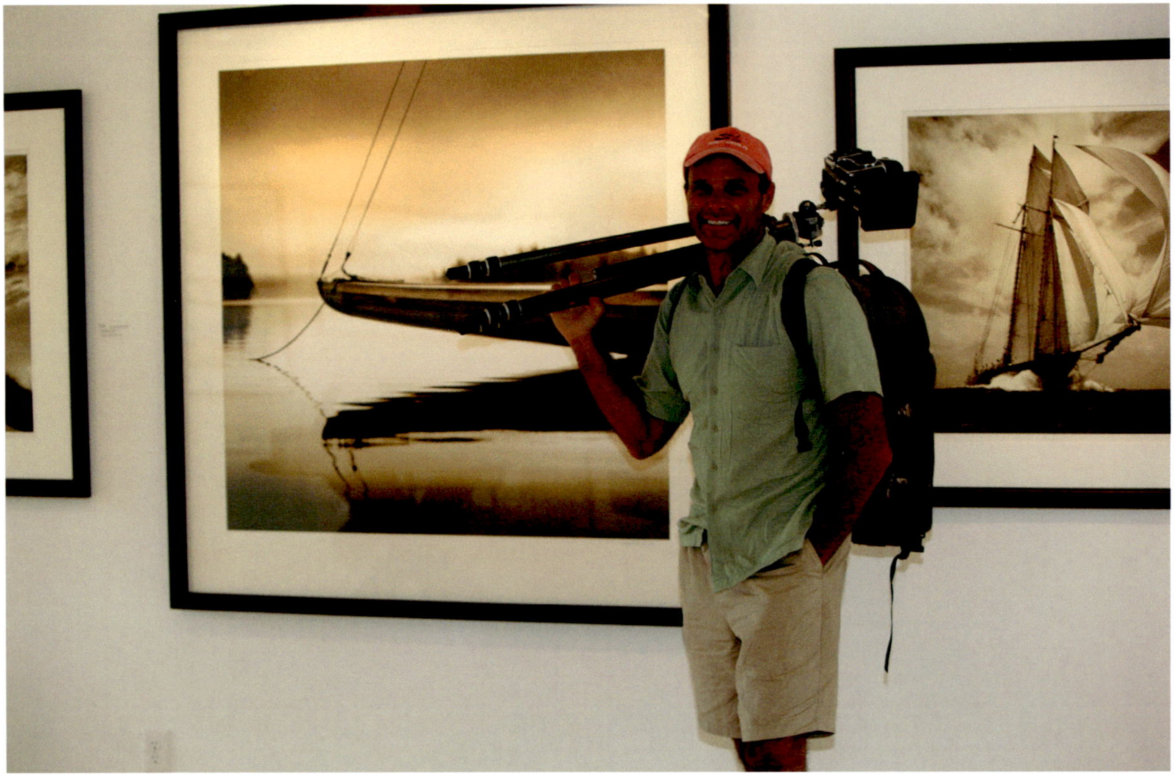

Photo Courtesy of Cindy Vallino, Focus Gallery, Chatham, MA

FOR MORE INFORMATION, PLEASE VISIT

WWW.MICHAELKAHN.COM

MICHAEL KAHN

Michael Kahn learned traditional photography in a portrait studio where they used Hasselblad cameras with a square 6x6 cm film format. Here, Michael received hands-on training in film handling and black-and-white printmaking. Michael continued on in advertising, product, and editorial photography.

In the mid-1990s, Michael took his first sailing photograph of a small boat in the fog on a lake in the Adirondacks, thus beginning his nautical photography career. Making the decision to stay with his film cameras instead of going with the new trends in digital equipment, he makes handmade photographs in his darkroom. Michael continues to travel the world, and his work is widely featured in magazines, museums, corporate and private collections, and fine-art galleries. Michael loves everything about nature and is interested in preservation. His other books are *Brandywine*, *The Spirit of Sailing*, and *Over the Dunes*.

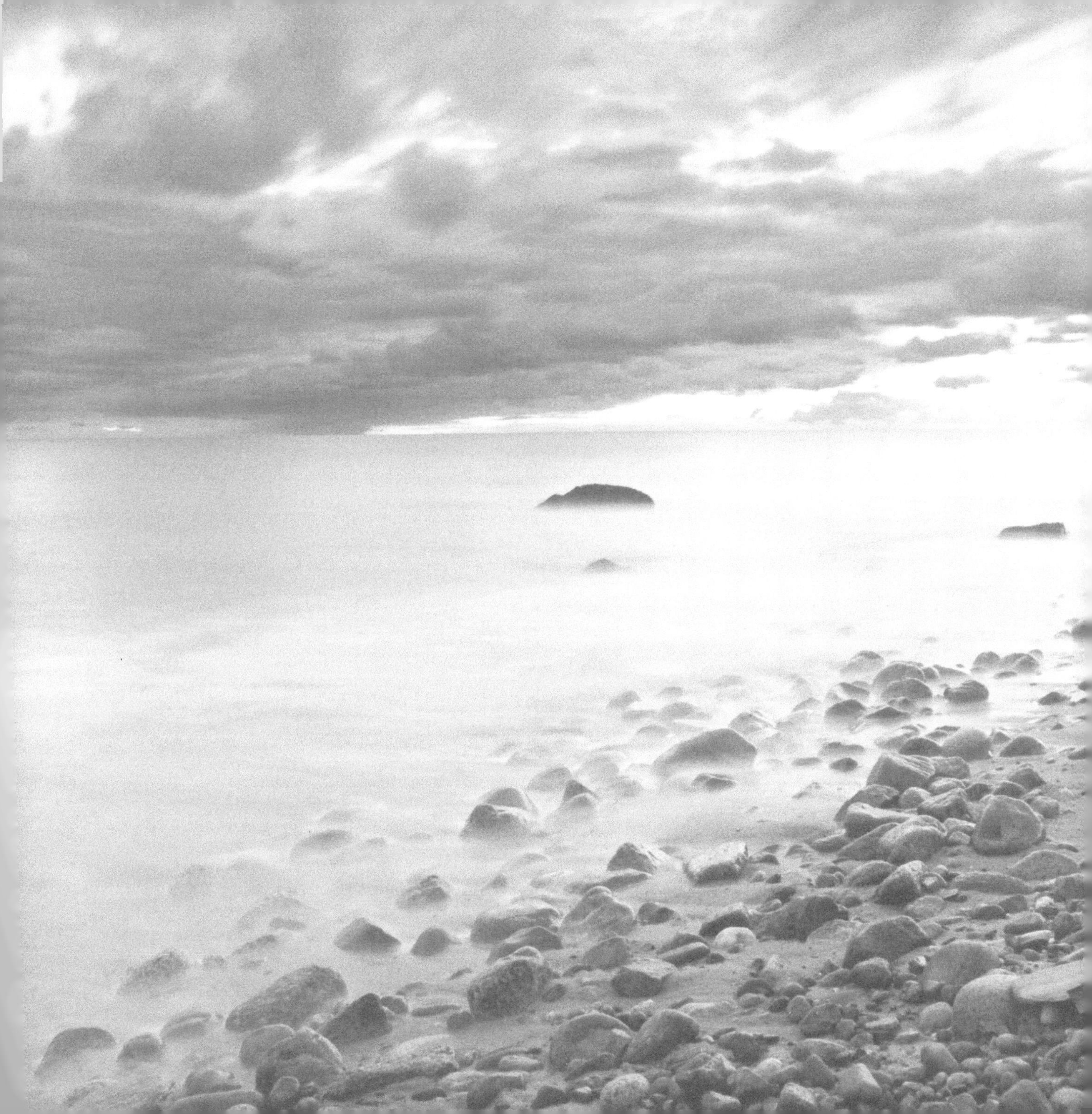

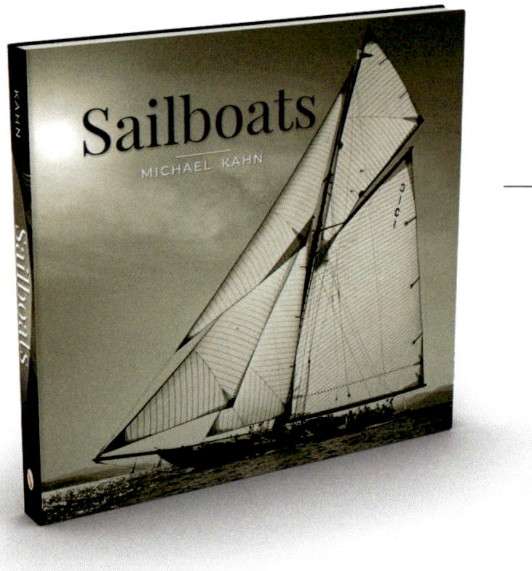

Other Schiffer Books by the Author:

Sailboats, ISBN 978-0-7643-5930-9

Other Schiffer Books on Related Subjects:

Archipelago New York, Thomas Halaczinsky
ISBN 978-0-7643-5507-3

Cape Cod along the Shore, Arthur P. Richmond
ISBN 978-0-7643-5160-0

Library of Congress Control Number: 2019947429

Designed by Danielle D. Farmer
Cover design by Danielle D. Farmer
Text by Michael Kahn and Christine Yurick
Creative design and input by Christine Yurick
Type set in Playfair Display/Montserratte

"A Momentary Creed" by W. S. Merwin, *The Shadow of Sirius* (Bloodaxe Books), reproduced with permission of Bloodaxe Books.

ISBN: 978-0-7643-5931-6
Printed in China

Published by Schiffer Publishing, Ltd.
4880 Lower Valley Road
Atglen, PA 19310
Phone: (610) 593-1777; Fax: (610) 593-2002
E-mail: Info@schifferbooks.com
Web: www.schifferbooks.com